ideals

Menus from Around the World
COOKBOOK

by Sophie Kay

What fun it is to be able to take a trip around the world . . . without ever leaving home . . . with our newest cookbook, MENUS FROM AROUND THE WORLD, as a guide.

Whether you want to try Wonton Soup . . . Chicken Enchiladas . . . or Danish Pastry . . . you will find a kitchen-tested recipe that is sure to please your family and friends. For the ultimate in truly elegant dining, treat your guests to any or all of the fourteen complete international menus!

Each menu has everything you will need to know to prepare and serve an entire meal . . . from appetizer to main dish to dessert. And, every menu is illustrated with beautiful color as well as black and white photography . . . with the usual touch here and there of poetry and prose . . . to make this another *ideals* cookbook which you will use and enjoy as you prepare meals that taste as good as they look.

And what fun you will have preparing and serving the best of international cuisine!

ISBN 0-89542-637-4 295

IDEALS PUBLISHING CORP., MILWAUKEE, WIS. 53201
© COPYRIGHT MCMLXXVI, PRINTED AND BOUND IN U.S.A.

An *ideals* Publication
Second Printing

CONTENTS

Traveling around the world
Is sure to be a treat
If everywhere you go, you find
Some special food to eat.

Perhaps you'd like to sail to France
To try a Chocolate Mousse
Or fly to Mexico for
Avocados Veracruz.

Or maybe it's some English food,
Like Steak and Kidney Pie,
Or Chinese food, like Wonton Soup,
That you would like to try.

But you don't have to travel to
The north, south, west and east—
Just step into your kitchen and
Prepare a foreign feast!

Beth Huwiler

ABBREVIATIONS

t.—teaspoon
T.—tablespoon
c.—cup
pkg.—package
pt.—pint
qt.—quart
oz.—ounce
lb.—pound

Pictured opposite
Wonton Soup, p. 4
Walnut Chicken, p. 5
Fried Pastries, p. 5

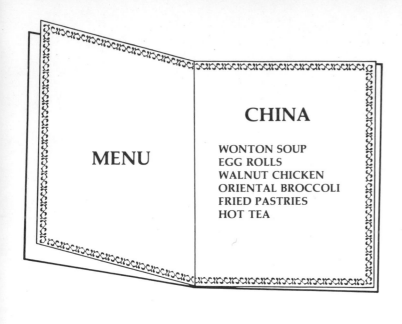

WONTON
Prepare, Cook & Serve: 2 hours

½ 10-oz. pkg. chopped frozen spinach
1 lb. ground pork
1 t. salt
1 T. soy sauce
1 t. minced ginger
1 egg
1 lb. ready-made wonton skins (about 50 pieces)

Thaw spinach and drain. Mix ground pork with salt, soy sauce and ginger. Add egg and spinach. Place 1 heaping teaspoon filling just below center of each wonton skin. Fold one side over the filling and tuck its edge under the filling. Roll up the filled cylinder, leaving ¼ inch of skin unrolled at the top. With a finger dipped in either water or beaten egg, moisten one end of the cylinder. Now take the 2 ends of the cylinder in the fingers of both hands and pull them until the ends meet and overlap ¼ inch. Pinch ends firmly together to seal. As each wonton is finished, place it on a plate and cover with a dry towel until ready to cook. At this stage Wonton can be frozen.

To cook: Boil 3 quarts water in a large pot; drop in wontons. Bring to boil again. Reduce heat to medium; cook about 6 minutes. Drain and serve in Wonton Soup.

6 to 8 servings
Can be frozen

NOTE: Wontons may also be served alone on a platter, sprinkled with soy sauce. Serve hot.

WONTON SOUP
Cook & Serve: 15 minutes

3 c. chicken broth
Salt
Soy sauce
1 c. fresh spinach leaves, chopped
12 prepared Wontons, cooked
½ c. thin slices cooked meat for a garnish (optional)
½ c. sliced mushrooms

Bring broth to boil; add salt and soy sauce to taste. Add chopped spinach and cooked Wonton. Heat and serve garnished with sliced mushrooms, cooked meat slices if desired.

4 servings
Can be frozen

MENU

CHINA

WONTON SOUP
EGG ROLLS
WALNUT CHICKEN
ORIENTAL BROCCOLI
FRIED PASTRIES
HOT TEA

EGG ROLLS
Prepare & Serve: 1¼ hours

½ lb. chicken breast, minced
½ lb. shrimp, minced
8 green onions, minced
1 T. vegetable oil
1 c. chopped bean sprouts
½ c. finely chopped water chestnuts
1 T. grated fresh ginger root
1½ T. soy sauce
1 lb. Egg roll skins (6½ x 7-inches)
Sweet-Sour Sauce

Sauté chicken, shrimp and onion in hot oil. Stir-fry 3 minutes. Add bean sprouts, water chestnuts, ginger root and soy sauce.

To make rolls, spread 1 tablespoon filling along one side of each skin. Fold over ends of skin and roll up like jelly roll, folding in ends. Seal rolls with a little water. Fry in hot fat (370°) for about 6 minutes or until skin is crisp, bubbly and brown. Cut each roll in 3 pieces. Serve as an appetizer with Sweet-Sour Sauce.

About 20 rolls
Can be frozen

SWEET-SOUR SAUCE
Cook & Serve: 15 minutes

½ c. brown sugar   ½ c. cider vinegar
2 T. cornstarch   2 T. soy sauce
1½ c. pineapple juice

Combine all ingredients in small saucepan. Cook over medium heat about 10 minutes or until sauce is thick and clear.

About 2 cups
Can be frozen

WALNUT CHICKEN (HOP TO GAI KOW)

Prepare & Serve: 45 minutes

3 large whole chicken breasts, boned
¼ c. vegetable oil
1 c. walnut halves or large pieces
1 t. monosodium glutamate
1 5-oz. can bamboo shoots, drained
4 t. cornstarch
¾ c. chicken broth
2 T. soy sauce
　Hot cooked rice

Remove skin from chicken breasts. Cut chicken into 1-inch squares. Heat oil in skillet; add walnuts and toast lightly. Remove walnuts; set aside. Add chicken to skillet and sprinkle with monosodium glutamate. Stir-fry over high heat for 3 minutes. Add bamboo shoots; continue stirring over high heat for 2 minutes. Blend cornstarch with chicken broth and soy sauce; add to skillet and mix well. Reduce heat; cover and simmer 4 to 5 minutes, until chicken is tender and sauce is thickened. Add toasted walnuts. Serve with hot cooked rice.

6 servings
Can be frozen

ORIENTAL BROCCOLI

Cook & Serve: 20 minutes

6 medium-size fresh broccoli stalks
　Vegetable oil
1 clove garlic, split
½ c. thinly sliced sweet red pepper
3 green onions with tops, sliced diagonally in ½-inch pieces
2 to 3 T. soy or teriyaki sauce
　Salt
　Toasted sesame seeds

Thinly slice broccoli stems, discarding tougher portions of stalk. Separate flowerets. Pour into a heavy frying pan enough oil to cover bottom. Heat thoroughly. Add garlic and broccoli stems. Cover and cook quickly until partially tender, stirring occasionally. Add broccoli flowerets and cook until just tender, but still crisp. Stir in red pepper and green onions; heat through. Season with soy or teriyaki sauce and salt. Garnish with sesame seeds.

6 servings
Cannot be frozen

CUCUMBER SALAD

Prepare: 10 minutes
Chill: 30 minutes

3 medium cucumbers
½ t. salt
1 T. sugar
1 t. soy sauce
1 T. vinegar
2 t. sesame oil or vegetable oil
　Pinch monosodium glutamate

Peel cucumbers; cut lengthwise in two. Remove seeds from center of each half cucumber. Cut into ¼-inch slices. Mix together salt, sugar, soy sauce, vinegar, oil and monosodium glutamate. Pour over cucumbers. Mix well; chill. Serve cold.

6 servings
Cannot be frozen

FRIED PASTRIES

Prepare & Serve: 1 hour

¾ c. chopped dates
¼ c. water
¼ c. granulated sugar
　Dash salt
¾ c. chopped almonds
1 8-oz. tube refrigerated crescent dinner rolls
1 egg yolk
1 t. water
2 t. sesame seeds
　Vegetable oil

Combine dates, water, sugar and salt; simmer until thick, stirring frequently. Cool; stir in almonds. Open package of rolls and unroll half carefully, without separating at perforations. Place unrolled dough on lightly floured board. Fold one rectangle of dough over the other, so that perforations are in opposite directions. Roll dough to a very thin rectangle, 7 x 14 inches. Cut in half, then cut each half into four 3½-inch squares. Place a rounded teaspoonful of filling on each. Moisten edges of dough; fold dough in half over filling and shape into crescent. Repeat with second half of package. Beat egg yolk lightly with water. Brush over pastries; sprinkle with sesame seeds. Heat fat to 360°. Fry pastries, a few at a time, about 4 minutes, turning frequently. Drain on paper toweling. Serve warm.

16 pastries
Can be frozen

5

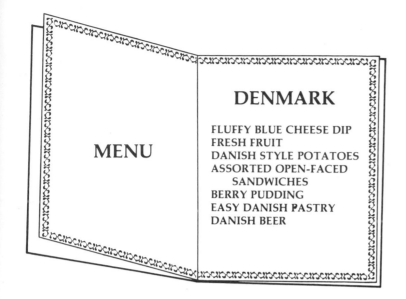

DENMARK

FLUFFY BLUE CHEESE DIP
FRESH FRUIT
DANISH STYLE POTATOES
ASSORTED OPEN-FACED
SANDWICHES
BERRY PUDDING
EASY DANISH PASTRY
DANISH BEER

MENU

Fluffy Blue Cheese Dip

FLUFFY BLUE CHEESE DIP
(ROQUEFORT DYP)
Prepare & Serve: 20 minutes

1 13-oz. pkg. Danish Blue cheese, crumbled or 2 c. firmly packed
¾ c. whipping cream
3 T. cream sherry
  Slivered almonds
  Assorted fruits

In mixing bowl, blend together crumbled blue cheese, ¼ cup whipping cream and sherry. Beat until light and creamy. Whip ½ cup whipping cream until soft peaks form; gently fold into blue cheese mixture. Chill one hour. Garnish with almonds. Use fruits, such as melon balls, grapes and kiwi, for dipping.

About 3 cups
Can be frozen

NOTE: You might also try this dip on a fresh fruit salad or serve with fresh apple or pears as a continental dessert.

FAIRYLAND FANTASY
Prepare & Serve: 15 minutes

1 slice brown bread
  Soft butter
  Lettuce leaves
3 or 4 slices boiled ham
2 cooked prunes
2 t. cream cheese
1 thin slice orange

Spread bread with butter. Place lettuce leaves on bread. Arrange boiled ham on lettuce, folding and overlapping slices. Top with prunes that have been stuffed with cream cheese. Place twisted orange slice between prunes.

Cannot be frozen

DANISH STYLE POTATOES
(KARTOFLER)
Cook & Serve: 45 minutes

6 large potatoes
½ c. butter
1 large onion, sliced
1 T. sugar
1 T. vinegar
1 t. salt
  Dash white pepper

Boil potatoes, cool, peel and slice ¼ inch thick. Set aside. Melt butter in frying pan. Add sliced onion; sauté 5 minutes, stirring occasionally. Add potatoes; sauté 5 minutes, turning potatoes to brown both sides. Add sugar, vinegar, salt and pepper; mix. Cook 5 minutes longer.

12 servings
Can be frozen

Assorted Open-Faced Sandwiches
Berry Pudding

COPENHAGEN CLOVERLEAF
Prepare & Serve: 25 minutes

1 slice brown bread
Soft butter
Lettuce leaves
5 to 7 slices salami
3 slices cucumber
3 slices hard-cooked egg
Pimiento
Parsley

Spread bread with butter. Place lettuce on bread; top with 2 to 4 slices of salami laid flat, then 3 slices folded and arranged in cloverleaf pattern. Top with slices of cucumber and hard-cooked egg. Garnish with pimiento and parsley.

Cannot be frozen

ROYAL ROAST BEEF
Prepare & Serve: 15 minutes

1 slice brown bread
Soft butter
Lettuce leaves
3 to 5 slices rare roast beef
3 bacon curls
2 T. egg salad
Thin tomato wedges
Thin green pepper wedges

Spread bread with butter. Place lettuce leaves on bread; top with 3 to 5 slices roast beef. Arrange 3 bacon curls in diagonal row across top. Put 1 tablespoon egg salad in each space between curls. Garnish with tomato and green pepper wedges.

Cannot be frozen

MERMAID'S MEDLEY
Prepare & Serve: 10 minutes

1 slice brown bread
Soft butter
Lettuce leaves
4 or 5 medium slices rare roast beef
3 spears cooked asparagus
Sieved hard-cooked egg yolk
Capers
Radish

Spread bread with butter. Place lettuce on bread; arrange roast beef on top of lettuce. Add asparagus; garnish with egg yolk, capers and radish.

Cannot be frozen

JUTLAND JUBILEE
Prepare & Serve: 10 minutes

1 slice brown bread
Soft butter
Lettuce leaves
1 T. horseradish
3 T. cream cheese
3 slices chopped ham, luncheon meat or honey loaf
3 thin wedges apple
Lemon juice
Mayonnaise
Chopped nuts

Spread bread with butter. Arrange lettuce leaves on bread. Blend horseradish with cream cheese; spread on meat. Form slices of meat in rolls and place on lettuce leaves. Separate rolls with apple wedges that have been dipped in lemon juice. Garnish with mayonnaise and chopped nuts.

Cannot be frozen

BERRY PUDDING
Prepare, Chill & Serve: 2 hours 20 minutes

2 10-oz. pkgs. frozen raspberries or strawberries
2 T. sugar
2 T. cornstarch
¼ c. cold water
½ t. vanilla
Sour cream or whipped cream

Thaw berries; place in blender; blend 1 minute. Berries may also be pureed by pressing them through a fine sieve. Place pureed berries in 2-quart saucepan. Add sugar; bring to boil, stirring constantly. Blend cornstarch and cold water; stir into fruit. Boil 1 minute. Remove from heat; stir in vanilla. Chill. Spoon over sliced pound cake or serve topped with sour cream or whipped cream.

About 2 cups
Can be frozen

PORK DELIGHT
Prepare & Serve: 15 minutes

1 slice brown bread
Soft butter
Lettuce leaves
4 slices cooked pork
2 T. potato salad
2 green pepper rings
1 pimiento-stuffed olive
1 carrot curl

Spread bread with butter. Place lettuce leaves on bread; top with 2 slices cooked pork. Add 2 diagonally folded slices, pointing them in opposite directions. Put 2 tablespoons potato salad in center, slip 2 green pepper rings under folds of top slices of pork. Garnish with stuffed olive and carrot curl.

Cannot be frozen

EASY DANISH PASTRY
(WIENER BRØD)

Mix, Shape & Bake: About 4 hours

1½ c. milk
2 pkgs. dry yeast
½ c. water
7½ c. all-purpose flour
2 eggs
½ c. sugar
½ c. shortening
2 t. salt
Grated rind of 1 lemon
1 t. lemon juice
1 c. soft butter or margarine
1 egg white, slightly beaten
Confectioners' Sugar Glaze
Chopped nuts

Scald milk; cool to lukewarm. Dissolve yeast in warm water (110-115°). Add milk and 3 cups flour. Beat until smooth. Stir in eggs, sugar, shortening, salt, lemon rind and juice. Sprinkle ½ cup flour on pastry cloth for kneading. Mix remaining flour into batter. Turn out dough onto floured cloth; knead until smooth and elastic. Place in greased bowl. Turn dough to lightly grease top. Cover; let rise 20 minutes. Roll in rectangle ⅓ inch thick. Dot ⅔ of dough with ¼ cup butter. Fold unbuttered portion of dough over half of buttered portion; fold over on other portion, making 3 thicknesses. Press edges together. Cover; let rise 20 minutes. Repeat rolling, dotting with butter, folding and rising 3 times, rolling dough in opposite direction each time. After last rising period, roll dough in rectangle ⅓ inch thick. Cut in desired shapes. Place on cookie sheet. Cover; let rise until doubled. Brush with egg white. Bake in preheated 400° oven 15 to 20 minutes. Brush warm pastries with Confectioners' Sugar Glaze. Sprinkle with nuts.

4 to 5 dozen
Can be frozen

CONFECTIONERS' SUGAR GLAZE

2 T. water
½ t. vanilla or orange extract
1 c. confectioners' sugar, sifted

Stir water and vanilla into sugar; mix well.

TO SHAPE DANISH PASTRY

Figure 8: Cut strips of dough ½ inch wide and 6 inches long. Hold 1 end of strip firmly in one hand; twist the other end, stretching it slightly until the two ends when brought together will naturally form a figure 8. Pinch ends together.

Knots: Cut strips as for figure 8; twist. Tie knot in center of each strip.

Rings: Cut strips as for figure 8; twist and shape into rings.

Snails: Cut strips as for figure 8. Hold one end of twisted strip down on cookie sheet; wind strip loosely around center; tuck end underneath.

Braids: Cut 3 strips ½ inch by 6 inches; press strips together at one end; braid. Cut braid in half; fasten ends well, making two small braids.

*Foldovers: Cut dough in 3-inch squares. Fold 2 opposite corners to overlap at center; press to seal.

*Four Point Stars: Cut dough into 2- or 3-inch squares. From each corner cut dough almost to center of square. Bring 2 opposite points to center; press down firmly.

*Nut or Cheese Filling may be used to fill Foldovers or Four Point Stars before baking.

NUT FILLING

½ c. chopped walnuts
3 T. sugar
½ t. cinnamon

Combine all ingredients and place a small amount in center of each Danish to be filled.

CHEESE FILLING

3 oz. cream cheese, softened
2 T. sugar
¼ t. vanilla

Combine all ingredients and place a small amount in center of each Danish to be filled.

Roast Ribs of Beef
Yorkshire Puddings
Peas with Cheese
Cranberry Crown Salad

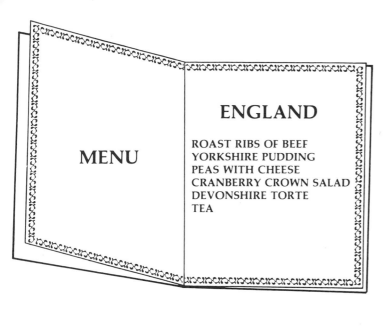

MENU

ENGLAND

ROAST RIBS OF BEEF
YORKSHIRE PUDDING
PEAS WITH CHEESE
CRANBERRY CROWN SALAD
DEVONSHIRE TORTE
TEA

ROAST RIBS OF BEEF
Roast: 23 to 35 minutes per pound

2 to 3-rib beef standing rib roast
Salt
Pepper
Yorkshire Pudding

For easier carving, have the retailer remove the chine bone and tie roast. Season meat with salt and pepper. Place roast, fat side up, on a rack in an open roasting pan. Insert meat thermometer so bulb reaches center of the thickest part, making sure that bulb does not rest in fat or on bone. Do not add water or cover. Roast in 325° oven to the desired degree of doneness. Meat thermometer will register 140° for rare; 160° for medium; 170° for well-done. Allow 23 to 25 minutes per pound for cooking roast to rare, 27 to 30 minutes for medium and 32 to 35 for well-done. Roasts are easier to carve if allowed to stand 20 to 30 minutes after they are removed from oven. Since roasts continue to cook during this standing period, it is best to remove the roast when the thermometer registers about 5 degrees below the temperature desired. About 15 minutes before roast is done, increase oven temperature to 400°. Heat muffin tin for Individual Yorkshire Puddings. Remove roast from oven and spoon off about ¼ cup clear hot beef drippings for use in puddings.

Allow ⅓ pound per serving
Can be frozen

INDIVIDUAL YORKSHIRE PUDDINGS
Mix & Bake: 45 minutes

1 c. sifted all-purpose flour
¾ t. salt
2 eggs
1 c. milk
¼ c. drippings from roast ribs of beef

Heat a large muffin tin in 400° oven for 5 minutes. Sift together flour and salt. Beat eggs. Add milk; slowly beat in dry ingredients. Spoon ½ teaspoon of beef drippings in each of the 12 hot muffin cups. Divide batter equally, approximately 2½ tablespoons in each cup. Bake in preheated 400° oven 30 minutes or until puddings are golden brown. Serve with roast. Heat remaining juices in roasting pan and serve over puddings, if desired.

12 individual puddings
Cannot be frozen

PEAS WITH CHEESE
Prepare & Serve: 15 minutes

3 10-oz. pkgs. frozen peas
6 T. butter
8 ozs. Cheddar cheese, cubed

Prepare peas according to package directions. Toss hot peas with butter and cheese cubes.

8 to 10 servings
Can be frozen

CRANBERRY CROWN SALAD
Prepare: 30 minutes
Chill: Overnight

4 c. cranberry juice
1 c. water
3 3-oz. pkgs. orange-flavored gelatin
⅛ t. salt
1 11-oz. can mandarin oranges, drained
1 small stalk celery, thinly sliced
1 unpeeled apple, diced
¼ c. slivered almonds

Combine 2 cups cranberry juice with 1 cup water in saucepan. Heat to simmer; add hot liquid to orange gelatin gradually, stirring constantly. When gelatin is completely dissolved, add salt and remaining 2 cups cranberry juice. Chill until slightly thickened. Carefully fold in oranges, celery, apple and almonds. Pour into a lightly oiled 6-cup mold. Chill overnight.

10 to 12 servings
Cannot be frozen

11

SOUR DOUGH ENGLISH MUFFINS

Mix and Let Stand: Overnight
Mix & Grill: 1¾ hours

5 to 6 c. all- purpose flour	2 t. salt
2 c. milk	1 t. baking soda
½ c. Starter	2 T. vegetable oil
2 T. sugar	1 pkg. dry yeast
	Cornmeal

Place 2 cups flour, milk, Starter, sugar, salt and baking soda in large mixing bowl (not metal); beat until smooth. Cover loosely with waxed paper; let stand in warm place (80 to 85°) at least 18 hours. Add oil and yeast; stir until well blended. Mix in more flour to make a moderately stiff dough. Turn onto lightly floured board and knead until smooth and elastic, 8 to 10 minutes. Sprinkle board with cornmeal. Roll dough ⅜ inch thick. Cut out muffins with floured cutter. Cover; let rest at room temperature until doubled, about 45 minutes. Bake muffins slowly on a lightly greased preheated 275° griddle or skillet 10 to 15 minutes on each side, turning once. To serve, split and toast.

18 3-inch muffins
Can be frozen

STARTER

2 c. all-purpose flour   2 c. warm water
1 pkg. dry yeast

Combine ingredients in large mixing bowl (not metal). Mix together until well blended. Let stand uncovered in warm place (80 to 85°) for 48 hours; stir occasionally. Stir well before using. Pour out required amount and replenish remaining starter by mixing in 1 cup each flour and warm water. Let stand uncovered in a warm place a few hours until it bubbles again. Then cover loosely and refrigerate. Use and replenish every two weeks.

DEVONSHIRE TORTE

Mix, Shape & Bake: 45 minutes

2 c. all-purpose flour
¼ c. sugar
1 T. baking powder
1 t. salt
⅓ c. shortening
½ c. chopped pecans
1 egg
1 egg, separated

1 c. dairy sour cream
2 to 6 T. milk
2 T. sugar
2 3-oz. pkgs. cream cheese, softened
1 21-oz. can cherry pie filling

Stir together flour, ¼ cup sugar, baking powder and salt. Cut in shortening until mixture resembles coarse crumbs. Stir in pecans. Beat egg and egg yolk together; blend in ½ cup sour cream and 2 tablespoons milk. Add all at once to flour mixture; stir until dry ingredients are moistened. If necessary, blend in more milk to make a soft dough. Turn onto lightly floured surface and knead gently for 30 seconds. Divide dough into 2 portions, one larger than the other. Place each portion on an ungreased baking sheet; roll out to circle ½ inch thick. Beat egg white until frothy; brush over dough. Sprinkle with 2 tablespoons sugar. Bake in preheated 425° oven 12 to 15 minutes or until golden brown. Remove from baking sheets; cool. Blend together cream cheese and remaining ½ cup sour cream; reserve 1 rounded tablespoon of this mixture for garnish. Place large scone on serving plate. Spread with cream cheese mixture; top with pie filling. Cover with small scone. Garnish with reserved cream cheese mixture.

8 to 10 servings
Can be frozen

Devonshire Torte

Steak and Kidney Pie

STEAK AND KIDNEY PIE
Prepare & Bake: 2¼ hours

1 lb. beef round steak, cut ¾ to 1 inch thick
1 beef kidney
¼ c. flour
1 t. salt
⅛ t. pepper
3 T. vegetable oil
1 medium onion, chopped
¼ c. chopped pimiento
2 T. Worcestershire sauce
¼ t. thyme
1½ c. water
Pie crust mix for 1 crust pie

Cut round steak in ¾- to 1-inch cubes. Wash kidney and remove tubes and fat; cut into ¾- to 1-inch cubes. Combine flour, salt and pepper; dredge steak and kidney cubes (reserving any extra flour). Heat oil in large frying pan. Brown meat; remove from pan.

Add onion to drippings; cook slowly until golden. Pour off drippings. Add pimiento, Worcestershire sauce, thyme and water to onion in frying pan; bring to boil. Stir in browned meat cubes and any remaining seasoned flour. Roll pastry to about ⅛-inch thickness. Invert 9-inch pie plate over pastry and cut a circle about an inch larger than rim of plate for top crust. Cut a design in crust to allow steam to escape. Cut a second circle inside the first about 1 inch from edge. This will give you a circular pastry strip to line the edge of the pie plate. Moisten edge of plate and top with outer circle of pastry, adjusting to fit. Turn meat mixture into pie plate and cover with top crust. Seal top pastry to edge and flute. Bake in preheated 325° oven 1½ hours.

6 servings
Can be frozen

Beef Stew Francaise
French Bread

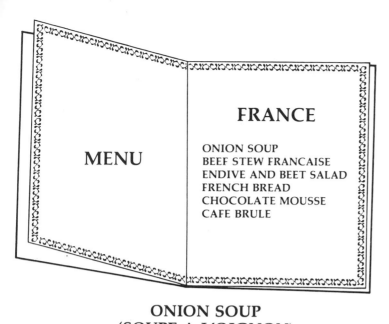

MENU

FRANCE

ONION SOUP
BEEF STEW FRANCAISE
ENDIVE AND BEET SALAD
FRENCH BREAD
CHOCOLATE MOUSSE
CAFE BRULE

ONION SOUP
(SOUPE A L'OIGNON)
Cook & Serve: 40 minutes

½ c. butter or margarine
8 medium onions, thinly sliced
2 T. flour
1 t. salt
   Freshly ground pepper
2 qts. beef broth
8 thick slices French bread
½ c. grated Parmesan cheese
½ c. shredded Gruyere cheese

Melt butter in large heavy pan. Add onions and sauté until golden; stir occasionally. Stir in flour and cook several minutes. Add salt and pepper. Pour in broth, stirring constantly. Bring to boil; lower heat and simmer, partially covered, about 20 minutes. Toast bread slices in oven until brown. Preheat broiler. Place toasted bread in ovenproof soup tureen or individual bowls. Sprinkle bread with Parmesan cheese. Pour soup over bread; top with Gruyere cheese. Brown under broiler until cheese begins to melt; serve immediately.

8 servings
Can be frozen

BEEF STEW FRANCAISE
(RAGOÛT DE BOEUF)
Cook & Serve: 2½ hours

3 lbs. boneless beef, cut into 1½-inch pieces
⅓ c. flour
2 t. salt
¼ t. pepper
3 T. vegetable oil
3 c. water
2 short celery stalks with leaves

4 sprigs parsley
1 bay leaf
1 large onion
6 whole cloves
¼ t. thyme
8 small whole potatoes
3 medium carrots, cut diagonally in 2-inch pieces
5 celery stalks without leaves, cut in 1½-inch pieces
1 10-oz. pkg. frozen peas
½ lb. fresh mushrooms, sliced
1 t. salt
   Flour for gravy

Dredge meat in ⅓ cup flour, mixed with 2 teaspoons salt and pepper. Brown in oil. Pour off drippings. Add water. Make *bouquet garni* by tying together celery stalks with leaves, sprigs of parsley and bay leaf. Stud one large onion with cloves. Add *bouquet garni*, clove-studded onion and thyme to stew meat. Cover tightly; cook slowly for 1 hour. Remove *bouquet garni* and clove-studded onion. Add potatoes, carrots and celery; cook 45 minutes. Add peas and mushrooms; sprinkle with 1 teaspoon salt. Cover; cook 15 to 20 minutes or until meat is tender and vegetables are done. Remove meat and vegetables to heated serving dish. Thicken cooking liquid with flour for gravy.

8 servings
Can be frozen

ENDIVE AND BEET SALAD
(SALADE)
Prepare: 20 minutes
Chill: 1 hour

1 lb. endive
¾ c. beets, shoestring style, well drained
½ c. French dressing
   Lemon juice to taste

Wash endive, pull apart and break into pieces. Place in ice water to crisp. Drain well and store in refrigerator until serving time. Combine beets with French dressing and lemon juice in a salad bowl. Chill 1 to 2 hours. Just before serving, add prepared greens to beets and dressing in bowl. Toss well. Taste; correct seasoning if necessary.

8 servings
Cannot be frozen

FRENCH BREAD
(PAIN FRANCAIS)
Mix, Shape & Bake: 3½ hours

½ c. buttermilk
2 pkgs. dry yeast
1½ c. warm water (110-150°)
6½ to 7 c. sifted all-purpose flour
2 T. sugar
1½ t. salt
2 T. soft shortening
Yellow cornmeal

Heat buttermilk to lukewarm. Remove from heat. (Separation does no harm.) Add yeast to water in large bowl; let stand 5 minutes. Stir. Add ½ the flour, buttermilk, sugar and salt. Beat about 100 strokes, or until smooth. Add more flour a little at a time with shortening. Mix in first with a spoon; then turn onto floured board and continue working the flour in until the dough is quite stiff. Cover. Let rest 10 minutes. Knead until smooth. Place in lightly greased bowl, twirling dough to grease all sides. Cover; let rise in warm place until double, about 1 hour. Dent will remain when finger is pressed deep into side of dough. Punch dough down; let rest 15 minutes. Divide dough in 2 parts. To shape loaf: Pat ½ dough into 6 x 12-inch rectangle. Starting at wide side, roll up tightly. Pinch edges of dough into roll; turn seam side to bottom. Taper ends by placing palms of hands on sides of each shaped piece of dough. Roll back and forth on board. Sprinkle cornmeal on cookie sheet. Place loaves, seam side down, 3 inches apart on baking sheet. Let rise in warm place until almost doubled, about 45 minutes. Make 4 diagonal slashes ¼ inch deep on top of each loaf. Brush with warm water. Just before baking brush loaves again with warm water. Bake in preheated 400° oven 35 to 45 minutes. Remove and cool on rack.

2 loaves
Can be frozen

CHATEAUBRIAND
Cook & Serve: 30 minutes

1½ to 2 lbs. center portion of beef
    tenderloin
Salt
Pepper
Bearnaise Sauce
Sautéed mushrooms

Preheat broiler. Place steak on rack in broiler pan so top of steak is 5 inches from heat. Broil 15 minutes, season with salt and pepper, turn; broil second side 10 to 15 minutes or to desired doneness. Season with salt and pepper; carve in slightly diagonal slices and serve with Bearnaise Sauce and mushrooms.

3 to 4 servings
Can be frozen

BEARNAISE SAUCE
Cook & Serve: 30 minutes

½ c. dry white wine
2 T. tarragon vinegar
2 small green onions, chopped
2 sprigs parsley, chopped
1 t. crushed dried tarragon
¼ t. coarsely ground black pepper
3 egg yolks, beaten
½ c. butter, melted
2 t. lemon juice
¼ t. salt
2 dashes cayenne pepper

Combine wine, vinegar, onions, parsley, tarragon and black pepper in top of double boiler. Cook until mixture is reduced to half (approximately ⅓ cup). Cool and add gradually to beaten egg yolks, stirring to blend. Return to pan and cook over hot (not boiling) water, stirring constantly until thick and creamy. Remove from hot water. Beat in butter, a small amount at a time; stir in lemon juice, salt and cayenne pepper.

1 cup
Can be frozen

CHOCOLATE MOUSSE
(MOUSSE AU CHOCOLAT)
Prepare: 45 minutes
Chill: 1 hour

4 oz. semisweet chocolate
4 egg yolks
4 T. butter
2 T. Grand Marnier
4 egg whites
¼ c. sugar

Place chocolate in saucepan. Cover with very hot water (about 2 inches deep). Put cover on pan; let stand about 5 minutes to soften chocolate. Test with the back of a fork to see if chocolate is soft. Carefully pour off water (some water may cling to the chocolate). Stir in yolks, one at a time, using wire whisk. Cook over low heat until thick. Remove from heat. Blend in butter, 1 tablespoon at a time, and Grand Marnier. Cool slightly.

Beat egg whites until soft peaks form; then add sugar 1 tablespoon at a time. Beat until stiff peaks form. Pour chocolate into large mixing bowl. Beat ¼ of stiffly beaten egg whites into chocolate mixture with a wire whisk; mix well. Fold in remaining whites with rubber spatula.

Pour into glass serving bowl or 6 individual small bowls. Chill about 1 hour or until serving time. Garnish with whipped cream and serve with crisp vanilla cookies.

6 servings
Cannot be frozen

NOTE: You can substitute 1 teaspoon vanilla for the Grand Marnier.

Chateaubriand

FLAMING FRENCH COFFEE
(CAFE BRULE)
Prepare: 15 minutes

2 sugar cubes
2 pieces lemon peel
2 whole cloves, heads removed
1 small stick cinnamon
⅓ c. brandy
⅔ c. strong coffee

Place sugar cubes, lemon peel, cloves, cinnamon stick and brandy in bowl. Blend well. Set aflame; let mixture burn for a minute or so, stirring constantly. Add strong coffee; strain into demitasse cups.

2 servings

BASIC CREPES
Mix & Cook: 1 hour
Chill: 2 hours

3 T. butter
3 eggs, slightly beaten
½ c. milk
½ c. water
¾ c. all-purpose flour
⅛ t. salt
Butter
Cottage Cheese Filling
Strawberry Sauce

Melt butter in 8-inch crepe or omelette pan. Pour butter into mixing bowl, set pan aside. To mixing bowl add eggs, milk and water; beat with rotary beater. Blend in flour and salt until mixture is smooth. Refrigerate batter 2 hours or overnight. Place buttered crepe pan over medium-high heat until hot enough to sizzle a drop of water. For each crepe pour 3 tablespoons or scant ¼ cup batter in pan, rotating pan as batter is poured. Crepes should set a thin lacy pancake almost immediately. If too much batter is poured into pan, pour off excess immediately. If there are holes, add a drop or two of batter for a patch. Cook until lightly browned on bottom; turn and brown other side. It may be necessary to add more butter to grease pan before pouring in batter for each crepe. Stack crepes between sheets of paper toweling or waxed paper until ready to use. Spread 3 tablespoons Cottage Cheese Filling down center of each crepe; fold the two sides over the center. Serve with Strawberry Sauce.

12 to 14 crepes
Can be frozen

Note: Allow 2 to 3 crepes per serving.

To freeze: Leave crepes between sheets of waxed paper; wrap in foil.

To reheat in oven: Remove waxed paper, wrap in foil and heat in preheated 325° oven about 15 minutes.

COTTAGE CHEESE FILLING
Mix: 10 minutes

3 c. small curd cottage cheese
3 T. sugar
1 t. grated lemon peel
½ t. vanilla

Blend together cottage cheese, sugar, lemon peel and vanilla. Use to fill crepes.

3 cups
Cannot be frozen

STRAWBERRY SAUCE
Cook: 15 minutes

3 c. fresh strawberries
½ c. sugar
¼ c. water
1 T. cornstarch
Dash salt
1 t. butter

Wash and hull strawberries; crush 1 cup. Slice remainder and set aside. Combine crushed berries, sugar, water, cornstarch and salt. Cook over medium heat, stirring constantly, until mixture thickens and boils. Boil and stir 1 minute. Add butter; fold in sliced berries.

About 2 cups
Can be frozen

Basic Crepes

CHEESE SOUFFLÉ
Mix & Bake: 1½ hours

Butter
Grated Parmesan cheese
2 T. butter
4 T. flour
1 c. cold half and half
½ t. salt
⅛ t. nutmeg
⅛ t. white pepper
5 jumbo egg yolks
½ c. grated Parmesan cheese
6 jumbo egg whites, room temperature
¼ t. cream of tartar
3 drops yellow food coloring
1 drop red food coloring

Coat 6-cup soufflé dish with butter. Sprinkle with grated Parmesan cheese. Melt 2 tablespoons butter in saucepan; stir in flour. Cook a few minutes. (Do not brown flour.) Stir in cold half and half. Add salt, nutmeg and pepper, cooking until thick. Remove from heat. Beat egg yolks with wire whisk; stir some of hot sauce into beaten yolks. Mix well and stir yolks into sauce. Add cheese and mix. Cover until you complete the remaining steps for the soufflé. Soufflé can be prepared up to this point several hours ahead.

Preheat oven to 350° If sauce was made hours ahead, heat over very low heat. As it heats, start by stirring in the center and gradually work your way to the sides, blending the sauce and not breaking it into pieces. Heat only to lukewarm and remove from heat. Beat egg whites with cream of tartar until stiff but not dry. Do not overbeat or whites will break down. Use a rubber spatula and keep whites pushed away from the sides into the center. When the large bubbles disappear, add the food colorings and beat until stiff. (Color whites to match the sauce; otherwise they dilute the yellow color of the soufflé. Uncolored whites not blended into the sauce also show up as white patches.) With a wire whisk, stir about 1 cup of the whites into the sauce. Use a rubber spatula to fold in the remaining whites. Pour into prepared soufflé dish. Bake in preheated 350° oven 40 to 45 minutes. Serve immediately as is or with Creole Sauce.

4 servings
Cannot be frozen

Variation: To make Broccoli Soufflé, fold one 10-ounce package frozen chopped broccoli, cooked and drained, into mixture after folding in egg whites. Bake in preheated 350° oven 40 to 45 minutes.

CREOLE SAUCE
Cook: 30 minutes

½ c. chopped green pepper
¼ c. chopped onion
¼ c. chopped pimiento-stuffed olives
1 clove garlic, minced
2 T. butter
1 10¾-oz. can tomato soup
¼ c. milk
3 sprigs parsley, chopped
¼ t. pepper
½ bay leaf, crushed
Pinch of thyme

Sauté green pepper, onion, olives and garlic in butter 5 minutes. Add remaining ingredients; mix well. Cover; simmer 15 minutes.

2 cups
Can be frozen

Cheese Soufflé

21

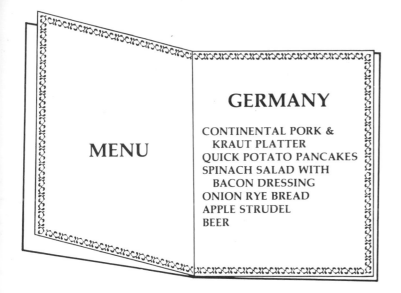

GERMANY

CONTINENTAL PORK &
KRAUT PLATTER
QUICK POTATO PANCAKES
SPINACH SALAD WITH
BACON DRESSING
ONION RYE BREAD
APPLE STRUDEL
BEER

MENU

Quick Potato Pancakes

CONTINENTAL PORK AND KRAUT PLATTER (SCHWEINESCHULTER UND KRAUT PLATTE)
Cook & Serve: 3 hours

2 to 3 lb. smoked pork shoulder roll
2 to 3 lb. boneless Boston-style pork shoulder roast
3 c. water
1 c. dry white wine
1 27-oz. can sauerkraut, drained
2 medium-sized tart apples, cored and cut into 8 wedges each
24 pitted prunes
3 links smoked thuringer
3 links fresh bratwurst or knackwurst

Place smoked pork shoulder and Boston-style pork shoulder in large Dutch oven. Add water; cover tightly and simmer 2 hours. Remove meat and boil cooking liquid rapidly until it is reduced to about 2 cups. Add wine and sauerkraut, stirring to combine thoroughly. Place smoked pork shoulder and fresh pork shoulder on top of sauerkraut. Add apples, prunes, smoked thuringer and fresh bratwurst. Bring to boil. Reduce heat and cover; simmer 30 minutes. Remove smoked and fresh pork shoulder; carve in ½-inch slices. Arrange carved meat with sausage, sauerkraut and fruit on hot platter.

10 to 12 servings
Can be frozen

QUICK POTATO PANCAKES (KARTOFFELPUFFER)
Cook & Serve: 1 hour

3 eggs
2 T. flour
1 t. salt
Dash white pepper
1 T. minced onion
⅛ t. nutmeg
1 12-oz. pkg. frozen shredded hash brown potatoes, thawed
Butter
Applesauce

Thoroughly combine eggs, flour, salt, pepper, onion and nutmeg. Stir in potatoes. Heat butter in large skillet until bubbly. For each pancake, spoon ¼ cup mixture into skillet; flatten. Fry over medium heat until golden brown on both sides, turning once. Serve with applesauce.

About 8 pancakes
Can be frozen

Pictured opposite
Continental Pork & Kraut Platter
Onion Rye Bread
Spinach Salad

ONION RYE BREAD
(ZWIEBEL ROGGEN BROT)
Mix & Bake: 2½ hours

    3 c. all-purpose flour
2½ c. rye flour
    ¼ c. brown sugar
    2 pkgs. dry yeast
    2 t. salt
    1 envelope onion soup mix
1¼ c. water
    1 c. milk
    2 T. butter or margarine
    ½ t. caraway seed
        Melted butter or margarine

Stir flours together; in large bowl combine 1½ cups flour mixture, brown sugar, yeast and salt. Combine onion soup mix, water, milk, 2 tablespoons butter and caraway seed in saucepan. Stir and heat until warm (120 to 130°). Gradually add liquid to combined dry ingredients, beating at medium speed; scrape bowl occasionally. Add ¾ cup flour and beat at high speed 2 minutes. Stir in enough additional flour to make a soft dough (2 to 3 cups). Cover and let rise in warm place until doubled, 40 to 50 minutes. Stir dough down. Turn into well greased 2-quart casserole, brush with melted butter; let rise until doubled, 20 to 30 minutes. Bake in preheated 350° oven 50 to 60 minutes or until done. Remove from casserole; brush crust with melted butter. Cool on wire rack.

1 large round loaf
Can be frozen

GERMAN POTATO SALAD
(DEUTSCHER KARTOFFEL SALAT)
Prepare & Serve: 45 minutes

    6 strips bacon, diced
    2 T. flour
    3 T. sugar
1½ t. salt
    ½ c. vinegar
    ½ c. water
    8 medium-sized potatoes, cooked and sliced
    1 small onion, minced
    2 stalks celery, diced

In large frying pan cook bacon over low heat until crisp; drain. To bacon drippings add flour, sugar and salt; cook until bubbly. Stir in vinegar and water. Cook, stirring con-

stantly, until thick. Cook 10 minutes over low heat. Place ⅓ of potatoes, onion, celery and sauce in layers in serving dish. Repeat 2 more times. Serve warm.

6 to 8 servings
Cannot be frozen

APPLE STRUDEL
(APFEL STRUDEL)
Mix, Shape & Bake: 1 hour
Let Stand: 2 to 4 hours

DOUGH

    1 egg
        Lukewarm water
    ¼ t. salt
    2 T. butter, melted
    1 T. sugar
    ¾ c. plus 2 T. sifted all-purpose flour
    4 t. vegetable oil
        Filling
        Confectioners' sugar

Break egg into measuring cup. Add enough water to make ⅓ cup; mix. Combine salt, 1 tablespoon butter and sugar; stir in egg mixture. Add ¾ cup flour; mix to form soft dough. Sprinkle remaining flour on pastry cloth. Turn out dough; knead lightly with fingertips until flour is absorbed. Brush with 1 teaspoon oil. Cover with warm bowl. Let stand 2 to 4 hours. Pat into flat circle. Roll into 12-inch circle. Brush top with remaining oil. Using back of hand stretch dough from middle, until it is thin as tissue paper. Spread Filling over dough to one inch from edge. Roll like jelly roll; seal edge. Place in semicircle on cookie sheet, cut edge down. Brush top with remaining butter. Bake in preheated 400° oven 20 to 25 minutes. Cool; sprinkle with confectioners' sugar.

FILLING

    3 c. finely sliced cooking apples
    ½ c. sugar
    ¼ t. nutmeg
    ½ t. cinnamon
        Dash allspice
    ½ c. chopped walnuts
    ⅓ c. coarse dry bread crumbs
    ½ c. butter, melted

Mix together all ingredients.

8 servings
Can be frozen

SPINACH SALAD WITH BACON DRESSING (SPINAT SALAT)
Prepare & Serve: 30 minutes

6 slices bacon
3 hard-cooked eggs
½ lb. fresh spinach
1 small onion, thinly sliced
1 large tomato, diced
½ c. white vinegar
2 t. dry mustard
  Dash garlic powder
1 T. sugar
1 t. salt
½ t. pepper
  Radish slices

Chop and fry bacon until crisp. Remove from pan; drain on paper toweling. Reserve ½ cup bacon drippings. Chop 2 eggs. Slice remaining egg into ¼-inch slices for garnish. Tear spinach into bite-sized pieces; mix with bacon, chopped eggs, onion and tomato. Combine reserved bacon drippings with vinegar, dry mustard, garlic powder, sugar, salt and pepper. Bring to boil, stirring constantly. Pour over salad; toss. Garnish with sliced egg and radish slices. Serve immediately.

8 servings
Cannot be frozen

APPLE OR PEACH COFFEE CAKE (APFEL KUCHEN)
Mix & Bake: 3 hours

¾ c. milk
1 pkg. dry yeast
¼ c. water
3¼ c. sifted all-purpose flour
2 eggs
½ c. soft butter or margarine
½ c. sugar
½ t. salt
2 T. butter, melted and cooled
1 T. sugar
3 c. sliced apples or peaches
½ t. cinnamon
⅛ t. nutmeg
½ c. sugar

Scald milk; cool to lukewarm. Dissolve yeast in warm water (105°). Add milk. Stir in 1½ cups flour; beat until smooth. Cover; let rise until doubled, about 1 hour. Add eggs, one at a time, beating well after each. Stir in ½ cup butter, ½ cup sugar, salt and remaining flour. Beat well. Spread dough in greased 9 x 9 x 2-inch baking pan. Spoon 2 tablespoons butter and 1 tablespoon sugar over dough. Cover; let rise until doubled. Press apples or peaches into dough. Mix together cinnamon, nutmeg and ½ cup sugar. Sprinkle over fruit. Bake in preheated 375° oven 40 to 45 minutes.

9 servings
Can be frozen

GERMAN KRAUT SKILLET
Cook & Serve: 40 minutes

1 lb. frankfurters
¼ c. butter
1 medium apple, coarsely grated
1 medium potato, coarsely grated
2 t. caraway seed
2½ c. undrained sauerkraut
¼ c. water

Split frankfurters in half lengthwise. Melt butter in large skillet. Add franks; cook until lightly browned. Mix apple, potato and caraway seed. Arrange apple mixture on top of frankfurters. Top with kraut. Add water; cover and simmer 20 minutes.

4 servings
Can be frozen

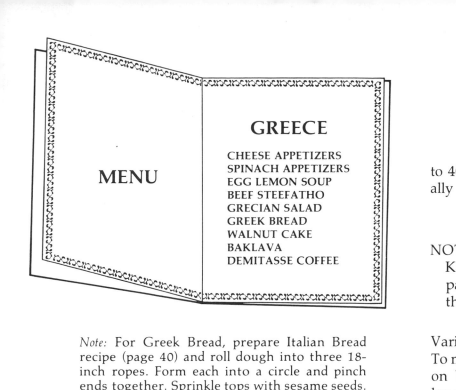

MENU

GREECE

CHEESE APPETIZERS
SPINACH APPETIZERS
EGG LEMON SOUP
BEEF STEEFATHO
GRECIAN SALAD
GREEK BREAD
WALNUT CAKE
BAKLAVA
DEMITASSE COFFEE

Note: For Greek Bread, prepare Italian Bread recipe (page 40) and roll dough into three 18-inch ropes. Form each into a circle and pinch ends together. Sprinkle tops with sesame seeds. Bake in preheated 425° oven 35 to 40 minutes or until golden brown.

CHEESE APPETIZERS
(TIROPITES)
Prepare & Bake: About 2½ hours

½ lb. Greek feta cheese, crumbled
1 8-oz. carton small curd cottage cheese with chives
2 eggs, slightly beaten
  Dash garlic salt
¼ t. salt
⅛ t. white pepper
½ lb. filo or strudel dough
½ lb. sweet butter, melted

To make filling: Combine all ingredients except filo and butter. Blend well and set aside. Take a sheet of filo and place it on a wooden board or tabletop; brush entire filo sheet generously with melted butter; add another sheet on top and brush with melted butter; continue this until you've used 5 filo sheets. Spread filling thinly over one-half of dough. Roll up like a jelly roll; place cut side down on baking sheet. Brush with melted butter; refrigerate about 15 minutes. With sharp knife, score chilled dough into diagonal pieces about 1 inch apart, cutting only about ⅛ inch through the dough. (Be sure not to cut all the way through to the filling before baking the rolls.) Bake only 2 rolls at a time on a baking sheet in a preheated 350° oven 35

to 40 minutes. Cool before cutting diagonally in 1-inch pieces. Heat before serving.

About 40 appetizers
Can be frozen before or after baking

NOTE: Strudel dough dries out quickly. Keep it covered with a sheet of waxed paper and slightly dampened towel over the waxed paper.

Variation for Cheese or Spinach Appetizers: To make triangle shapes, place one filo sheet on board. Brush with melted butter. Cut lengthwise into 5 equal strips. On each strip place 1 teaspoon Cheese or Spinach Filling about 1½ inches from left edge.

Fold opposite corner over filling, forming a triangle.

Continue folding triangle from left to right to the edge of each strip (corner to corner, as you would fold a flag) keeping the triangle shape. Brush with melted butter. Chill 15 minutes before baking. Bake in preheated 350° oven about 30 minutes or until golden brown.

About 65 to 75 appetizers

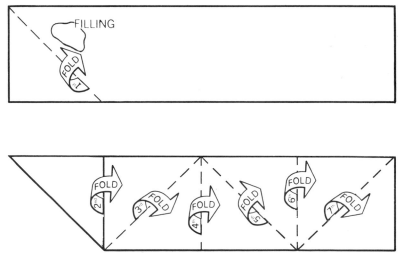

SPINACH APPETIZERS
(SPANAKOPITES)
Prepare & Bake: About 2½ hours

- 1 lb. fresh spinach
- 1 T. salt
- 4 green onions, chopped
- 1 T. olive oil
- 2 eggs, slightly beaten
- ¼ c. chopped parsley
- ¼ lb. Greek feta cheese, crumbled
- 3 T. Parmesan cheese
- ¼ t. pepper
- ½ lb. filo or strudel dough
- ½ lb. sweet butter, melted
  Dash salt

To make filling, wash spinach; discard coarse stems. Chop spinach in small pieces and place in colander. Sprinkle 1 tablespoon salt over spinach. Let stand ½ hour. Squeeze out excess water and place spinach in bowl to drain. Sauté onions in oil; add to spinach. Add eggs, parsley, cheeses and seasonings. Mix well. Prepare filo as for Cheese Appetizers. Spread spinach filling thinly over half the dough and complete same as Cheese Appetizers.

About 40 appetizers
Can be frozen before or after baking

GRECIAN SALAD
(SALATA)
Prepare & Serve: 25 minutes

- 1 clove garlic, cut in half
- 1 t. salt
- ⅛ t. pepper
- ½ c. olive oil
- ⅓ c. wine vinegar
- 1 T. lemon juice
- 1 T. oregano, crushed
- 1 small head lettuce, broken into bite-sized pieces
  Small wedge red cabbage, shredded
- ¼ bunch endive, thinly cut
- 3 green onions, thinly cut
- 3 tomatoes, cut into eighths
- 1 cucumber, quartered and thinly sliced
- ⅓ lb. feta cheese
- 6 ripe olives
- 6 anchovy fillets

Place garlic, salt, pepper, oil, vinegar, lemon juice and oregano in small jar with tight-fitting lid. Shake well. Toss vegetables together; add just enough dressing to coat greens. Crumble cheese and sprinkle over salad. Decorate top with olives and anchovies.

6 servings
Cannot be frozen

BAKLAVA
Prepare & Bake: About 3½ hours

- 2 c. finely chopped walnuts
- 2 T. sugar
- ½ t. cinnamon
- ⅛ t. cloves
- ⅛ t. allspice
- 1 lb. filo or strudel dough
- 1 lb. sweet butter, melted

In small bowl, combine all ingredients except filo dough and butter; set aside. Place a sheet of filo on a wooden board or tabletop; brush entire sheet generously with melted butter; add another filo on top and brush with melted butter. Continue this until you've used 5 filo sheets. Sprinkle filling thinly over half of dough. Roll up like a jelly roll; place cut side down on baking sheet. Brush with melted butter; refrigerate about 15 minutes. With sharp knife, score chilled dough into diagonal pieces about 1 inch wide, cutting only about ⅛ inch through the dough. (Be sure not to cut all the way through to the filling before baking the rolls.) Bake only 2 rolls at a time on a baking sheet in preheated 350° oven 45 minutes. Cool before cutting. When completely cooled, pour hot syrup over each roll. Let stand several hours or overnight before serving, so the syrup can penetrate the rolls. Finish cutting each roll and serve.

SYRUP

2 c. sugar	2 whole cloves
1 c. water	1 t. lemon juice
3 T. honey	2 T. brandy,
1 2-inch stick cinnamon	optional

Combine all ingredients except lemon juice and brandy in small saucepan. Bring to boil; simmer gently 8 minutes. Add lemon juice to syrup; simmer 2 minutes. Pour in brandy; simmer 1 minute. Remove spices; set aside.

About 60 pieces
Can be frozen before
or after baking

NOTE: If freezing baked Baklava do not pour syrup over rolls until they have been thawed.

EGG LEMON SOUP
(AVGOLEMONO SOUP)
Cook & Serve: 30 minutes

8 c. chicken broth
3 T. butter
1⅓ c. long grain white rice
1 t. salt
⅛ t. white pepper
3 eggs
Juice of 1½ large lemons
Chopped parsley

In a large saucepan, bring chicken broth and butter to boil over high heat. Stir rice, salt and pepper into hot broth; bring to boil again. Lower heat to simmer; cook until rice is tender. With electric mixer beat eggs until thick and light-colored, about 7 to 10 minutes; or process in blender on high speed until light and frothy. Add lemon juice to eggs, beating constantly. Pour in broth, a little at a time, beating until most of broth is used. Slowly pour this mixture back into the saucepan (with rice), stirring constantly. Sprinkle parsley over top of hot soup. Serve at once.

6 to 8 servings
Can be frozen

WALNUT CAKE
(KARITHOPETA)
Bake & Serve: 2 hours

1½ c. butter
1 c. sugar
6 eggs
½ c. milk
1 t. grated
  orange rind
2 c. sifted
  all-purpose flour
2 t. baking powder
¼ t. salt
1 t. cinnamon
2 c. medium
  chopped walnuts
Whipped cream
Orange wedges

Cream butter in large mixing bowl. Gradually add sugar; continue beating until light and fluffy. Add eggs, one at a time, beating well after each addition. Mix together milk and grated orange rind. Sift together flour, baking powder, salt and cinnamon. Add to creamed mixture alternately with milk and rind, beginning and ending with dry ingredients. Add nuts; mix well. Pour batter into greased 9 x 13 x 2-inch baking pan. Bake in preheated 350° oven 35 to 40 minutes. While hot, cut into diamond shapes and pour cold syrup over top. Cool 1 hour. Serve, garnished with whipped cream and orange wedges.

SYRUP

2 c. sugar
¼ c. honey
1½ c. water
1 t. lemon juice

Combine all ingredients together in small saucepan. Boil gently 4 to 5 minutes; cool.

12 servings
Can be frozen

BEEF STEEFATHO
Cook & Serve: 2½ hours

2 lbs. lean beef chuck or rump
⅓ c. olive oil
3 lbs. small onions
1 T. mixed pickling spices
1 small bay leaf
1 6-oz. can tomato paste
1¼ c. hot water
2 cloves garlic, minced
1 T. salt
¼ t. pepper
½ c. vinegar

Trim fat from meat and cut into 1-inch cubes. Place olive oil in Dutch oven over medium heat. Add meat and brown slowly, about 20 minutes. While meat is browning, peel onions, leave whole and set aside. Place pickling spice and bay leaf on 2-inch square of cheesecloth and tie securely. Mix together tomato paste and water. Add to meat with spice bag, garlic, salt and pepper. Place onions on top. Pour vinegar over all ingredients. (There should be enough liquid to half cover the contents of Dutch oven. If not, add more water.) Place heavy plate upside down on top of onions. Bring mixture to boil; cover and simmer 2 hours or until meat and onions are tender and liquid is reduced to a gravy. Remove spice bag before serving.

6 servings
Can be frozen

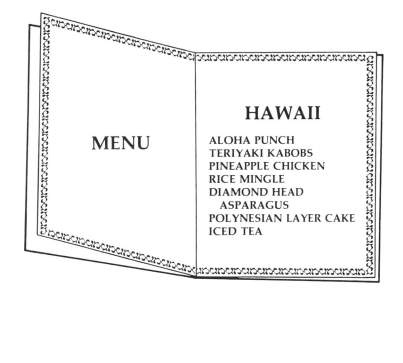

MENU

HAWAII

ALOHA PUNCH
TERIYAKI KABOBS
PINEAPPLE CHICKEN
RICE MINGLE
DIAMOND HEAD
  ASPARAGUS
POLYNESIAN LAYER CAKE
ICED TEA

ALOHA PUNCH

Prepare: 20 minutes
Freeze: Overnight

1 10 oz. pkg. frozen sliced peaches, thawed
1 10-oz. pkg. frozen mixed fruits, thawed
1 6-oz. can frozen orange juice concentrate
1½ c. water
2 T. lemon juice
6 thin lime slices
  Mint sprig
⁴⁄₅ qt. dry white wine, chilled
1 qt. Champagne or ginger ale, chilled

Combine undrained fruits, orange juice concentrate, water and lemon juice. Arrange some of fruit and lime slices in bottom of a 4¼-cup ring mold. Pour in enough juice mixture to barely cover fruits. Freeze until firm. Thoroughly chill remaining fruit and juice mixture. When bottom layer is frozen, pour on remaining mixture. Freeze until firm.

At serving time, pour wine and champagne into chilled punch bowl. Dip mold quickly in cold water. Unmold into punch bowl. Garnish ice ring with mint spring.

About 2 quarts

TERIYAKI KABOBS

Marinate: overnight
Prepare & Serve: 30 minutes

¼ c. soy sauce
½ t. chopped candied ginger
½ t. sugar
1 small clove garlic, pressed
1 lb. sirloin steak, 1 inch thick, cut into 24 cubes
24 1-inch fresh pineapple cubes
24 small stuffed green olives

Combine soy sauce, ginger, sugar and garlic. Add steak cubes; cover. Marinate overnight in refrigerator. Drain steak; place on wooden appetizer stick with pineapple chunk. Broil 3 inches from heat for 5 minutes; turn. Broil 3 minutes longer. Add olive to each stick; serve immediately.

24 appetizers
Cannot be frozen

Aloha Punch

Pictured opposite
Pineapple Chicken
Rice Mingle

PINEAPPLE CHICKEN
(HALAKAHIKI MOA)
Cook & Serve: 1¾ hours

    2 broiler-fryer chickens, cut into serving
      pieces
    1 t. monosodium glutamate
1½ t. salt
    1 egg, slightly beaten
    1 6-oz. can frozen pineapple juice
      concentrate, thawed and undiluted
1⅓ c. fine dry bread crumbs
    ¼ c. butter or margarine, melted
    1 3½-oz. can or 1⅓ c. flaked coconut

Rinse chicken pieces; pat dry with paper towel. Sprinkle monosodium glutamate and salt over both sides of chicken. Combine egg and pineapple concentrate in pie plate. Combine bread crumbs with melted butter in another pie plate; add coconut and mix well. Coat chicken pieces with pineapple mixture, then roll in coconut mixture. Place on 2 shallow foil-lined baking pans. Bake in 350° oven 40 minutes. Reverse pans in oven for even baking. Bake another 40 minutes. If chicken begins to brown too much before end of baking time, cover loosely with foil.

8 servings
Can be frozen

RICE MINGLE
(LAIKÍ)
Prepare & Serve: 45 minutes

Bibb lettuce
3 c. cooked rice, cooled
2 green peppers, chopped
2 pimientos, chopped
2 tomatoes, peeled and cubed
2 T. chopped onion
2 T. chopped parsley

Line serving dish with bibb lettuce. Combine remaining ingredients; toss with Dressing. Place in serving dish with lettuce. Chill.

8 servings
Cannot be frozen

DRESSING

¾ c. olive oil   ½ t. white pepper
¼ c. white wine   1 clove garlic,
  vinegar   minced
1½ t. salt

Combine all ingredients; blend thoroughly.

DIAMOND HEAD ASPARAGUS
Cook: 25 minutes

1½ lbs. fresh   ⅓ c. water
  asparagus   ½ t. seasoned salt
3 T. butter   2 t. soy sauce

Snap off and discard woody base of asparagus stalks. Slice diagonally into bite-size pieces. Melt butter in skillet. Add water, seasoned salt and soy sauce. When mixture boils, add asparagus; toss lightly. Cover; cook over medium-high heat for 3 to 5 minutes or until tender. Do not overcook.

6 to 8 servings
Can be frozen

POLYNESIAN LAYER CAKE
Mix & Bake: 1¼ hours

    ¾ c. butter or margarine
1½ c. sugar
    1 t. lemon extract
    1 t. vanilla
    3 c. sifted cake flour
    ½ t. salt
    4 t. baking powder
    1 c. milk
    5 large egg whites, stiffly beaten
      Whipped Cream Icing
      Flaked coconut

Cream butter; gradually add sugar, creaming until light and fluffy. Add extracts. Sift together flour, salt and baking powder. Add to creamed mixture alternately with milk. Fold in stiffly beaten egg whites. Turn into 3 greased and floured 9-inch layer pans. Bake in preheated 350° oven 25 to 30 minutes. When cool frost with Whipped Cream Icing; sprinkle with coconut.

12 servings
Can be frozen

WHIPPED CREAM ICING

1 t. unflavored   3 T. sugar
  gelatin   1 t. vanilla
2 T. cold water   1 pt. whipping cream

Soften gelatin in cold water 5 minutes; dissolve over hot water. Whip cream until stiff; beat in sugar and vanilla. Add cooled gelatin. Beat mixture until it forms peaks. Spread on cake.

ONÓ ONÓ PORK KABOBS
Cook & Serve: 1¼ hours

2 pork tenderloins (about 2 lbs.)	1 t. salt
	¼ t. ginger
3 slices fresh pineapple, cut ½ to ¾ inch thick	¾ c. orange juice
	2 T. dark molasses
	1 t. lemon juice
2 t. cornstarch	1 t. rum extract

Cut tenderloins crosswise into slices 1 inch thick (approximately 8 to 10 slices from each tenderloin). Cut each pineapple slice into six wedges. Combine cornstarch, salt and ginger in a small saucepan. Stir in orange juice, dark molasses and lemon juice. Cook over low heat, stirring until mixture thickens. Continue cooking, stirring occasionally, 2 to 3 minutes. Stir in rum extract. Alternately thread pieces of pork tenderloin (cut side up) and pineapple on four 12-inch skewers. Brush with sauce. Place 4 to 5 inches from heat. Broil, turning and brushing with sauce every 5 minutes, until done, 20 to 30 minutes.

6 servings
Cannot be frozen

LUAU COCONUT STRIPS
Prepare & Serve: 45 minutes

8 ½-inch slices pound cake
1 15-oz. can sweetened condensed milk
1 7-oz. pkg. flaked coconut

Remove crusts from cake. Cut slices into 3 strips. Dip cake strips in milk; roll in coconut. Broil on baking sheet about 4 inches from heat using medium heat, 5 to 8 minutes on first side or until lightly browned. Turn; broil 3 to 5 minutes on second side. Cool.

24 strips
Can be frozen

LEILANI SPARERIBS
Cook & Serve: 1 hour 40 minutes

4 to 6 lbs. spareribs
1 6-oz. can frozen pineapple juice concentrate, defrosted
2 T. soy sauce
1 T. instant minced onion

Place ribs on grill or on rack on broiler pan as far as possible from heat. Broil 1 hour and 15 minutes; turn occasionally. Combine pineapple juice concentrate, soy sauce and onion. Continue cooking 15 minutes, brushing with glaze and turning occasionally.

6 servings
Can be frozen

Pork Kabobs

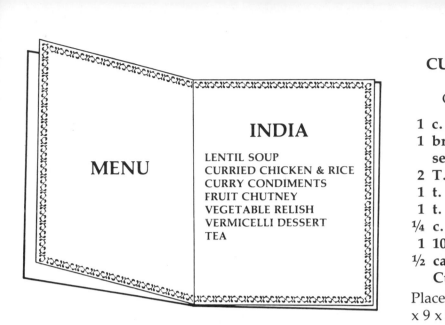

MENU

INDIA

LENTIL SOUP
CURRIED CHICKEN & RICE
CURRY CONDIMENTS
FRUIT CHUTNEY
VEGETABLE RELISH
VERMICELLI DESSERT
TEA

LENTIL SOUP
(PURPOO MULLIGATUNNY)
Cook & Serve: 2 hours 20 minutes

½ c. dried lentils
7 c. water
2 T. butter
1 small onion, chopped
1 clove garlic, minced
½ t. crushed dried red pepper
2 t. curry powder
1 t. lemon juice
1 t. salt

Wash lentils; discard any imperfect ones. Place in Dutch oven, cover with water. Bring to boil; boil 2 to 3 minutes and remove from heat. Let stand covered 1 hour. Drain; add to 7 cups boiling water; cook until soft, about 1 hour. Melt butter in separate saucepan. Add onions, garlic, red pepper and curry powder. Mix well; sauté 3 minutes over low heat, stirring constantly. Add to lentils. Stir in lemon juice and salt. Cook 15 minutes, stirring occasionally. If desired, lentils may be forced through a sieve or pureed in an electric blender.

6 to 8 servings
Can be frozen

CURRIED CHICKEN WITH RICE
(MOORGEE KARI)
Cook & Serve: 1 hour 20 minutes

1 c. rice, uncooked
1 broiler-fryer chicken, cut in serving pieces
2 T. butter
1 t. paprika
1 t. curry powder
¼ c. almonds, slivered
1 10½-oz. can chicken broth
½ can water
Curry Sauce

Place dry white rice in bottom of buttered 13 x 9 x 2-inch baking dish. Top with pieces of chicken. Dot with butter. Sprinkle with paprika, curry powder and almonds. Add chicken broth and water. Cover; bake in 375° oven 45 minutes. Remove from oven. Pour Curry Sauce over chicken; continue cooking 15 more minutes, uncovered.

CURRY SAUCE

1 10¾-oz. can cream of chicken soup
¼ c. milk
2 T. sherry
1 T. cornstarch
½ t. curry powder

Mix together ingredients in saucepan; bring to boil over low heat. Remove from heat.

4 servings
Can be frozen

CURRY CONDIMENTS
Prepare & Serve: ½ hour

¾ c. blanched halved almonds, toasted
½ c. shredded coconut
4 hard-cooked egg yolks, sieved

Arrange condiments in individual dishes. Condiments are almost as important as the ingredients in a curry. Choice is infinite. Tradition decrees chutney, chopped pickle, and coconut; but try raisins, chives, chopped ham, crumbled potato chips, kumquats, peanuts, chopped lemon or lime peel, orange marmalade, fresh scallions, radishes, chopped egg yolk or white, chopped green olives, or chopped bacon. Choose from the savory, sharp, sweet, pungent, salty, and tart. Serve each condiment in a separate small dish.

Pictured opposite
Curried Chicken with Rice

FRUIT CHUTNEY
Cook & Serve: 1¾ hours

1 c. cider vinegar
1⅓ c. firmly packed brown sugar
1½ t. salt
¼ t. crushed dried red peppers
1 t. cinnamon
1 t. chili powder
½ t. black pepper
½ t. cloves
½ t. coriander
1 t. ginger
2 small cloves garlic, minced
4 c. diced cooking apples (1 lb.)
1 c. chopped prunes (about ½ lb.)
1⅓ c. chopped dried apricots (about ½ lb.)

Mix together all ingredients in large heavy saucepan; bring to boil. Simmer over low heat 1 hour or until soft and brown. Stir frequently. Cool.

About 1½ pints
Can be frozen

VEGETABLE RELISH
(SAMBAL)
Prepare: 20 minutes
Let Stand: 1 hour

4 T. butter
2 medium onions, chopped
1 clove garlic, minced
¼ t. crushed dried red pepper
½ t. powdered ginger
1 t. turmeric
¼ t. ground cumin seed
2 small cucumbers, thinly sliced
2 small tomatoes, thinly sliced

Melt butter in saucepan. Add onions, garlic, red pepper, ginger, turmeric and cumin seed. Sauté over low heat 10 minutes; stir frequently. Divide mixture in half; place in two bowls. Add cucumber to one bowl and tomatoes to the other. Mix gently. Let stand one hour before serving. Serve at room temperature with curries.

6 servings
Cannot be frozen

VERMICELLI DESSERT
(PAYASAM)
Cook & Serve: 30 minutes

1 T. light seedless raisins
½ c. water
4 T. butter
⅓ c. cashew nuts
½ lb. vermicelli
2 c. milk
1 c. sugar
1 t. vanilla extract

Soak raisins in water 10 minutes. Drain well. Melt butter in saucepan. Add nuts and raisins; sauté 5 minutes stirring frequently. Remove nuts and raisins; set aside. Break vermicelli in half; place in saucepan. Brown lightly. Add milk; bring to a boil. Cook over low heat 8 minutes. Add sugar and vanilla; cook 2 minutes longer. Add nuts and raisins. Serve hot.

6 servings
Can be frozen

TURNOVERS
(SAMOSAS)
Mix, Shape & Cook: 2 hours

1¼ c. sifted all-purpose flour
1 t. salt
3 T. butter, melted
⅓ c. yogurt
Meat Filling
Potato Filling
Vegetable Oil

Sift together 1 cup flour and salt. Stir in butter and yogurt. Turn onto floured pastry cloth; knead gently to form dough, adding additional flour if needed. Cover with bowl; let stand 30 minutes. Roll as thin as possible; cut into 4-inch squares. Place heaping teaspoon of Meat or Potato Filling on each; moisten edges with water. Fold pastry over filling to form a triangle; press edges closed with finger or fork. Slit or prick tops. Heat oil to 375°. Deep fat fry several at a time 3 to 4 minutes or until browned, turning once. Drain on paper toweling; keep hot in 170° oven.

About 15 turnovers
Can be frozen

Turnovers

NOTE: Pastry may also be cut into 4-inch circles, folded and sealed the same as the triangles. Serving Variations: Serve with banana chips for a snack or with chutney for a light meal.

MEAT FILLING

1 clove garlic, minced
1 small onion, minced
2 T. butter, melted
½ lb. lean ground beef
1 medium tomato, chopped
1 t. salt
½ t. curry powder
   Dash cayenne pepper
   Few sprigs parsley, minced

Sauté garlic and onion in butter for 5 minutes. Add meat; cook over high heat until browned, stirring frequently. Add tomato, salt, curry powder, cayenne and parsley. Cook over medium heat 5 minutes. Drain any remaining liquid. Cool. Use to fill Samosas.

Fills 15 Turnovers

POTATO FILLING

8 oz. frozen French fried potatoes
½ c. frozen green peas
2 T. vegetable oil
½ t. mustard seed
1 small onion, minced
1 T. water
½ t. ground coriander
½ t. fennel seed
½ t. curry powder
½ t. ground ginger
¼ t. ground cumin
¼ t. ground turmeric
   Dash cayenne pepper

Thaw frozen potatoes and peas; cut French fries into ½-inch pieces. In a heavy 10-inch frying pan, heat oil; add mustard seed and cook till seeds begin to burst. Add onion and fry, stirring constantly, until golden. Stir in potatoes, peas, water and remaining spices. Cover and simmer, stirring occasionally, for 10 minutes or till potatoes and peas are fork-tender. Cool. Use to fill Samosas.

Fills 15 Turnovers

ITALY

MENU

ANTIPASTO
NOODLES ALFREDO
PIEDMONT VEAL CUTLETS
FRIED ZUCCHINI
TOMATO & CUCUMBER
  SALAD
ITALIAN BREAD
CANNOLI
CAPPUCCINO

ANTIPASTO
Prepare: 35 minutes
Chill: 2 hours

½ c. olive oil
⅓ c. wine vinegar
2 T. water
1 clove garlic, cut in half
¼ t. seasoned salt
   Dash freshly ground pepper
2 9-oz. pkgs. frozen artichoke hearts,
   halved
1 medium head lettuce
1 head bibb lettuce
4 hard-cooked eggs, sliced
   Slices of Provolone, Scamorze, Moz-
   zarella or Gorgonzola cheese
   Slices of Italian salami
12 pimiento stuffed olives
12 ripe olives
5 pimiento strips
   Anchovy fillets
1 T. chopped chives

Combine oil, vinegar, water, garlic and seasonings in small jar. Cover; shake well.
Chill. Cook artichokes according to package
directions; cool and drain. Remove garlic
from dressing. Pour over artichokes; chill 2
hours. Line a large platter with large leaves
of head lettuce. Break inner leaves and bibb
lettuce leaves into bite-sized pieces and
place in center of platter. Add chilled artichokes, reserving marinade. Pour marinade over lettuce. Arrange eggs, cheeses,
salami and olives around artichokes. Garnish with pimiento and anchovy fillets.
Sprinkle chives over all.

6 servings
Cannot be frozen

HOMEMADE EGG NOODLES
(FETTUCINE)
Mix & Serve: about 1 hour

2 c. all-purpose flour
1 egg
1 egg yolk
1 T. olive oil
1 t. salt
   About ¼ c. warm water

Place flour in large mixing bowl; make a well
in center and put in eggs, olive oil and salt.
Mix together with fingers until dough can be
gathered into a rough ball. Moisten with few
drops warm water and gather remaining
flour. Add more water if needed. Knead
dough on lightly floured board until smooth
and elastic, about 10 minutes. Add more
flour if dough seems sticky. Wrap in waxed
paper; let dough rest 10 minutes before rolling. Divide into 2 balls. Cover one with
waxed paper; place other ball on floured
board. Flatten dough with your hand; dust
with flour. Using rolling pin, roll paper-thin.
Sprinkle lightly with flour; let dough rest 10
minutes. Repeat with other ball of dough.
Carefully roll up each piece of dough like a
jelly roll. With a sharp knife, cut dough
crosswise in strips ¼ inch wide. Unroll each
strip and spread on waxed paper. Drop in 8
quarts rapidly boiling salted water. Cook 5 to
7 minutes, or until just tender (al dente).

NOTE: If noodles are not cooked at once;
   cover tightly with plastic wrap and store
   in refrigerator up to 24 hours.

6 to 8 servings
Can be frozen

NOODLES ALFREDO
(FETTUCINE ALFREDO)
Cook & Serve: ½ hour

1 recipe Homemade Egg Noodles or
1 8-oz. pkg. noodles
½ c. softened butter
½ c. grated Parmesan cheese
⅓ c. half and half or light cream

Cook noodles in 8 quarts boiling salted water
until tender, about 7 to 10 minutes. Drain
well. Place noodles in hot serving bowl.
Add butter, cheese and cream a little at a
time. Mix gently after each addition. Serve
immediately.

6 to 8 servings
Can be frozen

Pictured opposite
Antipasto
Noodles Alfredo
Piedmont Veal Cutlets
Tomato and Cucumber Salad
Italian Bread
Cannoli
Cappuccino

PIEDMONT VEAL CUTLETS
(VITELLO ALLA PIEMONTESE)
Cook & Serve: 1 hour

¼ c. butter
2 T. olive oil
1½ lb. veal cutlets, thinly sliced
⅔ c. dry white wine
1 t. salt
½ t. crushed oregano
½ t. crushed basil
1 T. dried parsley flakes
  Dash freshly ground pepper
  Sliced Provolone cheese

Heat butter and oil in large skillet; add veal cutlets and brown. Stir in wine, salt, oregano, basil, parsley flakes and pepper. Cook over low heat for about 15 minutes; baste frequently. Place cooked cutlets in shallow baking pan; pour sauce over all. Put Provolone over each cutlet. Bake in preheated 400° oven about 12 minutes or until cheese melts. Serve immediately.

6 servings
Can be frozen

TOMATO AND CUCUMBER SALAD
(INSALATA)
Prepare: 20 minutes
Chill: 1 hour

5 medium tomatoes, sliced
1 cucumber, scored and thinly sliced
1 green onion, thinly sliced
3 T. olive oil
2 to 3 T. red wine vinegar
½ t. salt
½ t. crushed oregano
¼ t. crushed basil
  Freshly ground pepper
1 T. minced parsley

Place tomato slices, cucumber slices, and green onion in glass bowl. Mix together remaining ingredients; pour over salad. Chill about 1 hour before serving.

6 servings
Cannot be frozen

ITALIAN BREAD
Mix, Shape & Bake: 3 hours

6 to 6½ c. all-purpose flour
2 pkgs. dry yeast
2 c. water
2 T. sugar
2 T. vegetable oil
2 t. salt
  Cornmeal
1 egg white
1 T. water

Stir together 2 cups flour and yeast. Heat water, sugar, oil and salt over low heat only until warm, stirring to blend. Add liquid ingredients to flour-yeast mixture and beat until smooth (about 2 minutes at medium speed or 300 strokes by hand). Add 2 cups flour and beat 1 minute on medium speed or 150 strokes by hand. Cover; let rise in warm place (80 to 85°) until light and bubbly, about 45 minutes. Stir down. Add more flour to make a moderately stiff dough. Turn onto lightly floured surface; knead until smooth and elastic, about 15 minutes. Shape into ball and place in lightly greased bowl; twirl to grease all sides. Cover; let rise in warm place until doubled, about 1½ hours. Punch down. Divide dough into 3 equal parts; shape into balls. Cover; let rest 10 minutes. Roll each portion of dough into 12 x 8-inch rectangle. Starting at 12-inch side, roll up jelly roll fashion. Seal seam. With side of hand, press ends to seal. Fold ends under loaf. Place on greased baking sheet sprinkled with cornmeal. Using sharp knife, make diagonal cuts about ⅛ inch deep across top of each loaf. Combine egg white and water; brush loaves with mixture. Let rise in warm place until doubled, about 45 minutes. Brush with egg white mixture again. Bake in preheated 425° oven 35 to 40 minutes, or until golden brown and done.

3 loaves
Can be frozen

FRIED ZUCCHINI
(ZUCCHINI FRITTI)
Cook & Serve: ¾ hour

2 lbs. zucchini, sliced ¼ inch thick
Salt
About 6 T. olive or vegetable oil
Flour
Grated Parmesan cheese

Lightly sprinkle zucchini slices with salt; let stand about 5 minutes. Heat oil in large skillet. Dip zucchini slices in flour. Sauté on both sides until lightly browned. Drain on paper toweling. Continue until all are finished. Sprinkle with grated Parmesan cheese. Serve hot.

6 servings
Cannot be frozen

CAPPUCCINO
Prepare & Serve: 15 minutes

2 c. cold water
2 T. sugar
¼ c. instant espresso coffee
½ c. whipping cream, whipped
Ground nutmeg

Bring water and sugar to boil. Add coffee; stir to dissolve. Pour into demitasse cups. Top with whipped cream. Sprinkle with nutmeg.

6 servings

Cannoli

CANNOLI
Prepare & Serve: About 1 hour

1½ c. sifted all-purpose flour
2 T. sugar
¼ c. shortening
1 egg yolk
¼ c. dry white wine
Vegetable oil
Cheese Filling
¼ c. chopped pistachio nuts
Confectioners' sugar

Sift together flour and sugar. Cut in shortening. Stir egg yolk into wine; add to flour mixture. Mix dough until stiff. Divide dough in half; roll out as thin as paper. Cut into 3½-inch squares. Place cannoli forms diagonally on pastry squares, from point to point. Draw remaining 2 corners loosely over cannoli form. Moisten underside of overlapping corner with wine; press corners together. Heat oil to 375°. Fry 2 to 3 minutes or until golden brown, turning occasionally, drain. Cool. Use pastry tube or teaspoon to fill shells with Cheese Filling. Sprinkle nuts on filling on each end. Dust center with confectioners' sugar.

About 25 shells
Can be frozen

NOTE: Cannoli forms can be made from ⅞-inch wide doweling cut into 5-inch lengths.

CHEESE FILLING

2 lbs. Ricotta cheese
1 c. sugar
1 t. vanilla
3 oz. sweet chocolate, broken into small pieces

Cream cheese and sugar until smooth. Fold in vanilla and chocolate.

Sukiyaki
Empress of the East Salad
Almond Bavarian

42

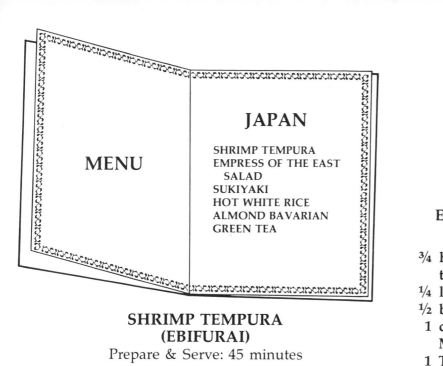

MENU

JAPAN

SHRIMP TEMPURA
EMPRESS OF THE EAST
 SALAD
SUKIYAKI
HOT WHITE RICE
ALMOND BAVARIAN
GREEN TEA

SHRIMP TEMPURA (EBIFURAI)

Prepare & Serve: 45 minutes

1 c. sifted all-purpose flour
½ t. salt
½ t. sugar
1 c. ice water
1 egg, slightly beaten
2 T. vegetable oil
1 lb. cooked shrimp
2 qts. vegetable oil
 Tempura Sauce
 Hot Mustard Sauce

Combine flour, salt and sugar. Add water, egg and 2 tablespoons oil; beat lightly. Heat 2 quarts oil to 375°. Dip shrimp into batter. Fry several pieces at a time in deep hot fat until golden brown, about 4 to 5 minutes. Drain on paper toweling. Keep fried shrimp warm in 170° oven while frying remaining pieces. Serve with Tempura Sauce and Hot Mustard Sauce for dipping.

8 servings
Can be frozen

TEMPURA SAUCE

½ c. chicken broth   2 T. dry sherry
2 T. soy sauce   ½ t. ginger

Combine ingredients. Bring to boil; cool.

About ¾ cups

HOT MUSTARD SAUCE

¼ c. boiling water   ½ t. salt
¼ c. dry mustard   2 t. vegetable oil

Stir water into mustard gradually. Add salt and oil.

½ cup

EMPRESS OF THE EAST SALAD

Prepare & Serve: 25 minutes

¾ head Chinese cabbage (about 3 c. torn)
¼ lb. spinach (about 3 c. torn)
½ bunch curly endive (about 2 c. chopped)
1 c. (4 oz.) cubed Swiss cheese
 Milk
1 T. toasted sesame seeds
2 medium-sized white turnips, pared and cut in julienne strips
 Cherry tomatoes
 Ginger Dressing

In a large bowl toss together chilled greens. Dip cheese in milk, then in sesame seeds to coat. Arrange cheese, turnips and cherry tomatoes on greens. Serve with Ginger Dressing.

8 servings
Cannot be frozen

GINGER DRESSING (SHOGA)

Prepare & Serve: 30 minutes

2 T. all-purpose flour
2 T. firmly packed light brown sugar
1 t. salt
1 t. ground ginger
 Dash cayenne pepper
1 c. milk
1 egg, beaten
¼ c. white wine vinegar
1 t. butter
1 c. dairy sour cream

Combine flour, sugar, salt, ginger and cayenne in 1-quart saucepan. Add milk to egg; gradually stir into flour mixture. Cook over medium heat, stirring constantly, until thick. Cool 1 additional minute. Gradually stir in vinegar then butter. Cool. Fold in sour cream.

About 2 cups
Cannot be frozen

SUKIYAKI
(SKEE-YA-KEE)
Prepare & Serve: 45 minutes

½ c. beef broth
¼ c. sugar
1 t. monosodium glutamate
1½ c. soy sauce
2 lbs. sirloin steak
2 T. vegetable oil
1 carrot
1 c. sliced fresh mushrooms
1 green pepper, thinly sliced
3 stalks celery, sliced diagonally
4 green onions, sliced diagonally
1 8-oz. can water chestnuts, drained and sliced
1 1-lb. can bean sprouts, drained
1 14⅔-oz. can bamboo shoots, drained
Hot White Rice

Heat beef broth; add sugar, monosodium glutamate and soy sauce. Mix well; set aside. Cut meat into slices, ¼ inch thick and 3 inches long. Using vegetable peeler, cut carrot lengthwise into thin strips; cut strips in half. Place large skillet over low heat for 3 minutes; add oil. Heat 1 minute. Brown meat slightly on both sides. Add half of sauce to meat. Push meat to one side of skillet. In separate wedges in skillet add carrot strips, mushrooms, green pepper, celery and onions. Cook 1 minute; toss-stir each vegetable with a spoon and fork during cooking. In separate wedges add water chestnuts, bean sprouts and bamboo shoots. Pour remaining sauce over vegetables. Heat 3 to 4 minutes. Serve with hot white rice or rice ring.

6 to 8 servings
Cannot be frozen

HOT WHITE RICE
(GOHAN)
Prepare & Serve: 25 minutes

1 c. rice
2 c. water
1 t. salt

Wash and drain rice. Put water and salt in saucepan. Bring to boil. Add rice. Reduce to simmer; cook 15 to 20 minutes or until all water is absorbed. If desired, serve Sukiyaki in a rice ring. Pack rice firmly into a buttered 6-cup ring mold; unmold immediately. To keep mold warm if not used immediately, cover tightly with aluminum foil and place in a covered skillet filled with 1 inch hot water. Place over very low heat.

6 servings
Can be frozen

ALMOND BAVARIAN WITH
APRICOT SAUCE
(AMONDO AWAYUKIKAN)
Prepare: 30 minutes
Chill: 5 hours

1 T. unflavored gelatin
¼ c. sugar
Dash salt
2 egg yolks, slightly beaten
1¼ c. milk
½ t. almond extract
2 egg whites
¼ c. sugar
1 c. whipping cream, whipped
Apricot Sauce
Toasted slivered almonds

In a saucepan combine gelatin, ¼ cup sugar and salt. Mix together egg yolks and milk. Add to gelatin mixture; heat over low heat until gelatin is dissolved. Stir in almond extract; chill until mixture mounds slightly. Beat egg whites to soft peaks. Gradually beat in ¼ cup sugar until stiff peaks form. Fold into gelatin mixture. Fold in whipped cream. Turn into 8 individual molds (about 5 ounces each) or a 3-cup mold. Chill until set. Serve topped with Apricot Sauce and toasted slivered almonds.

8 servings
Cannot be frozen

APRICOT SAUCE
(ANZU SOSU)

1½ c. apricot nectar
½ c. sugar
1 t. fresh lemon juice
½ c. dried apricot halves, quartered

In saucepan combine apricot nectar, sugar and lemon juice. Add apricots: cover and simmer 20 to 25 minutes or until apricots are tender. Chill. Serve over Almond Bavarian.

About 1½ cups

TOKYO SALAD
Prepare & Chill: 1½ hours

10 oz. vermicelli
¾ c. mayonnaise
2 T. soy sauce
1 6½-oz. can small shrimp, minced
1 t. hot mustard
1 t. salt
¼ t. garlic powder
　 Dash white pepper
1 16-oz. can bean sprouts, drained
1 c. frozen green peas, thawed
1 stalk celery, diced
½ green pepper, diced
1 small onion, chopped
⅓ c. diced water chestnuts
1 4-oz. can sliced mushrooms
　 Lettuce leaves

Break vermicelli into 3-inch lengths. Cook in boiling salted water (2 quarts plus 1 tablespoon salt) until tender yet firm, about 7 to 11 minutes. Rinse in cold water; drain. In large bowl combine mayonnaise, soy sauce, drained shrimp, hot mustard, salt, garlic powder and pepper. Add vermicelli and remaining ingredients except lettuce. Cover and chill thoroughly. To serve, place about 1 cup of the vermicelli mixture on a crisp lettuce leaf.

8 servings
Cannot be frozen

Tokyo Salad

GINGER FRUIT ORIENTAL (SHŌGA KUDÁMONO)
Prepare: 15 minutes
Chill: 2 to 3 hours

1 1-lb. can sliced peaches, drained
1 c. orange juice
2 t. finely chopped candied ginger
2 bananas
　 Kumquats
　 Mint leaves

Combine peach slices, orange juice and candied ginger. Chill several hours to blend flavors. Peel bananas and run fork down sides to flute. Cut in diagonal slices. Add to peach mixture. Heap in serving dishes. Garnish with kumquats and mint leaves.

4 servings
Cannot be frozen

Chicken Enchiladas
Bean & Avocado Tostadas
Avocados Veracruz
Mexican Soufflé Surprises

AVOCADO DIP
(GUACAMOLE)
Mix: 15 minutes

- 3 peeled ripe avocados
- 2 T. minced onion
- 1 T. chili powder
- ½ t. salt
- 1 large ripe tomato, peeled, seeded and chopped
- ¼ c. French dressing
- Lemon juice
- Tortilla chips

Mash avocados; mix in onions and seasonings. Add chopped tomato and French dressing; mix until smooth. Sprinkle top with lemon juice to prevent discoloring. Serve chilled with crisp tortilla chips.

About 3 cups
Cannot be frozen

SOUTH-OF-THE-BORDER SALAD
Prepare & Serve: 20 minutes
Chill: 2 hours

- ½ c. vegetable oil
- ⅓ c. wine vinegar
- 1½ t. sugar
- 1 t. salt
- 1 t. chili powder
- 1 small clove garlic, pressed
- 2 qts. assorted salad greens
- 1 small cucumber, sliced
- 2 green onions, thinly sliced

In a small jar, combine all ingredients except greens, cucumber and onions. Chill several hours. Break greens into bite size pieces in wooden bowl. Add cucumber and onions. Toss with dressing.

8 servings
Cannot be frozen

CHICKEN ENCHILADAS
(ENCHILADAS CON PECHUGA DE POLLO)
Bake & Serve: 1 hour

- 2 3-oz. pkgs. cream cheese
- 1 T. vinegar
- ⅓ c. dairy sour cream
- 3 whole cooked chicken breasts, shredded
- 1 t. prepared mustard
- ¼ t. salt
- ⅛ t. garlic powder
- ¼ c. pitted ripe olives, chopped
- ½ green pepper, chopped
- Tabasco
- Vegetable oil
- 8 corn tortillas
- 1 1-lb. can stewed tomatoes
- 1 8-oz. can tomato sauce
- 2 avocados
- ¾ c. shredded Cheddar cheese

Soften cream cheese with vinegar; mix in sour cream, shredded chicken, mustard, salt, garlic powder, olives, green pepper and a few drops tabasco. Heat about 1 tablespoon oil in skillet; sauté tortillas, one at a time, lightly on each side; add oil as necessary. Tortillas should not be crisp. Drain on paper towels. In same skillet, heat tomatoes and tomato sauce with 2 tablespoons oil and few drops of tabasco. Meanwhile, spoon chicken mixture onto centers of tortillas. Spoon about 1 tablespoon tomato mixture over chicken; roll up tortillas. Place in greased shallow 2-quart baking dish. Pour hot tomato mixture over top. Cover lightly with foil. Bake in preheated 400° oven 15 minutes. Meanwhile cut avocados lengthwise into halves; remove seeds and skin. Cut avocado lengthwise into slices; arrange on top of enchiladas. Sprinkle with Cheddar cheese. Return to oven about 3 minutes, until cheese melts. Serve at once.

6 servings
Can be frozen

BEAN AND AVOCADO TOSTADAS (TOSTADAS DE FRIJOLES GUACAMOLE)
Prepare & Serve: 50 minutes

8 corn tortillas
Vegetable oil
2 15-oz. cans Mexican-style chili beans
   or red kidney beans
1½ t. chili powder
3 avocados
2 T. lemon juice
2 green chiles, chopped
1 large tomato, chopped
⅛ t. garlic salt
Few drops tabasco
Lettuce
Dairy sour cream

Sauté tortillas in oil until crisp, turning once. Drain on paper towels. Keep warm on cookie sheet in warm oven. Drain beans reserving ½ cup liquid. In large skillet, mash beans with fork; mix in 6 tablespoons oil, chili powder and reserved bean liquid. Cook until mixture begins to bubble; continue cooking until all liquid and fat are absorbed. Keep warm. Cut avocados lengthwise into halves; remove seeds and skin. Mash avocados with lemon juice. Stir in chiles and tomato; add garlic salt and tabasco. Place lettuce leaves on individual serving plates. Top with tortillas. Spread bean mixture on tortillas. Mound with avocado mixture; top with sour cream. Serve at once.

4 or 8 servings
Cannot be frozen

PUFF PASTE ROLLS (HOJALDRE)
Mix, Chill & Bake: 2 hours

2 c. all-purpose flour
1 t. salt
½ c. butter, softened
1 T. lime juice
6 to 8 T. cold water
4 T. butter, softened
⅓ c. sugar
½ t. cinnamon

Sift together flour and salt. Cut in ½ cup butter until mixture resembles coarse crumbs. Stir in lime juice. Sprinkle with water, a tablespoon at a time, mixing lightly until dough begins to stick together. Press into ball; knead gently 30 seconds. Roll out on lightly floured surface to 14 x 8-inch rectangle. Dot with 1 tablespoon butter; spread as evenly as possible. Starting from the narrow edge, fold ⅓ of the pastry over center third; fold over remaining third, making 3 layers. Roll into 14 x 9-inch rectangle; spread with another tablespoon butter; fold as before. Roll, butter and fold pastry 2 more times. Place on baking sheet, roll into 14 x 9-inch rectangle and cover with plastic wrap. Chill thoroughly. Let pastry stand at room temperature 30 minutes. Cut into 1 x 3-inch bars. Pick up each bar and twist in center, making a half twist; place on greased baking sheet. Combine sugar and cinnamon; sprinkle over rolls. Bake in preheated 400° oven 20 to 25 minutes, or until golden brown.

42 rolls
Can be frozen

AVOCADOS VERACRUZ
Prepare & Serve: 30 minutes

3 avocados
Lemon juice
1 7½-oz. can crab meat
1 c. crushed corn chips
2 t. prepared mustard
1 t. chili powder
⅛ t. garlic powder
2 whole pimientos, chopped coarsely
¼ c. mayonnaise
¼ c. chopped parsley
Tabasco
Whole corn chips

Cut avocados lengthwise into halves; remove seeds and skin. Sprinkle avocados with lemon juice. In bowl mix crab, crushed corn chips, mustard, chili and garlic powders, pimiento, mayonnaise, parsley and 1 teaspoon lemon juice. Add tabasco to taste. Mound crab mixture into avocados. Serve with whole corn chips.

6 servings
Cannot be frozen

Puff Paste Rolls

MEXICAN STYLE COFFEE
(CAFE CON LECHE)
Prepare & Serve: 10 minutes

8 cups hot strong coffee
Hot milk
Sugar

To hot coffee, stir in desired amount hot milk. Add sugar to taste. To use instant coffee: bring milk to boil and add coffee to desired strength.

8 servings

MEXICAN SOUFFLÉ SURPRISES
Bake & Serve: 1¼ hours

1 4-oz. can green chiles	¼ t. cream of tartar
6 T. butter or margarine	8 2-inch squares Muenster cheese, ⅛-inch thick
¼ c. flour	2 15-oz. cans Spanish-style tomato sauce
½ t. salt	
⅛ t. paprika	
1 c. milk	¾ t. oregano
1 c. shredded American cheese	3 avocados
	Lemon juice
4 eggs, separated	5 to 5½ c. hot cooked rice

Discard seeds from chiles, then cut into eight 2 or 3-inch pieces; chop any remaining chiles. Melt 4 tablespoons butter in saucepan; stir in flour, salt and paprika. Heat until bubbly; stir in milk. Cook until thick. Remove from heat; stir in shredded American cheese. Beat egg whites with cream of tartar until stiff peaks form. With same beaters, beat yolks until thick. Gradually beat cheese mixture into yolks; fold into whites. Fill 8 greased 6-ounce custard cups half full. Place a piece of chile and Muenster cheese on each. Top with remaining egg mixture. Place cups in shallow pan filled to ½-inch depth with hot water. Bake in preheated 350° oven about 30 minutes or until wooden pick inserted into center comes out dry. Meanwhile heat tomato sauce with oregano and remaining butter and chopped chiles. Cut avocados lengthwise into halves; remove seeds and skin. Slice avocados crosswise; sprinkle with lemon juice. To serve, spoon rice on plates. Slide sharp knife around edge of custard cups; invert on rice and lift off cups. Arrange avocado slices around soufflés. Drizzle with tomato mixture; pass remainder.

8 servings
Cannot be frozen

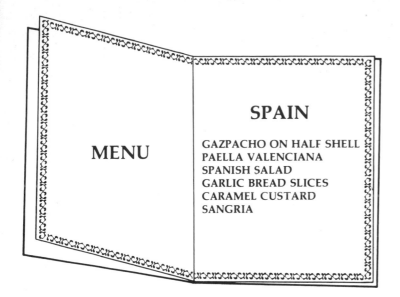

MENU

SPAIN

GAZPACHO ON HALF SHELL
PAELLA VALENCIANA
SPANISH SALAD
GARLIC BREAD SLICES
CARAMEL CUSTARD
SANGRIA

SPANISH SALAD
(ENSALADA A LA MURCIANA)
Prepare: 35 minutes
Chill: 2 hours

- 1 clove garlic, halved
- 1 small head lettuce, shredded
- 1 small green pepper, diced
- 1 cucumber, peeled and diced
- 1 small onion, chopped fine
- 2 large tomatoes, peeled, seeded and chopped
- ¼ c. olive oil
- ¼ c. wine vinegar
- 1 T. lemon juice
  Dash sugar
- ½ t. dried dillweed, crushed
- ⅛ t. pepper
- ¾ t. salt

Rub wooden salad bowl with garlic halves; discard garlic. Place shredded lettuce on bottom of bowl. Sprinkle with a layer of diced green pepper, then layers of diced cucumber, chopped onion and tomatoes. In small jar with cover, mix together remaining ingredients. Shake and pour dressing evenly over entire salad. Cover; chill 2 to 3 hours before serving.

8 servings
Cannot be frozen

COLD SOUP OR SALAD
(GAZPACHO ON HALF SHELL)
Prepare: 30 minutes
Chill: 4 hours

- 4 large ripe tomatoes
- 1 cucumber
- 1 stalk celery, chopped
- ½ green pepper, chopped
- 1 small onion, chopped
- 4 T. olive oil
- 2 T. red wine vinegar
  Few drops tabasco sauce
- 1 t. salt
- 1 garlic clove
  Avocados (optional)
  Fresh lemon juice (optional)

Remove skins from tomatoes; chop fine. Peel and chop cucumbers. Mix together tomatoes and cucumbers with celery, green pepper, onion, olive oil, vinegar and seasonings. Crush garlic and mix in. Chill at least 4 hours. Serve in chilled bowls. If you wish to serve Gazpacho in avocado shells, cut avocados lengthwise into halves. Remove seeds and skin. Sprinkle with fresh lemon juice. Fill halves with Gazpacho.

8 servings
Cannot be frozen

Gazpacho

Pictured opposite
Paella Valenciana

PAELLA VALENCIANA
Prepare & Serve: 1¾ hours

⅓ c. olive oil
2½- to 3-lb broiler-fryer, cut in small
　　pieces
1 t. salt
¼ t. pepper
2 large tomatoes, peeled, seeded and
　　finely chopped or 1-lb. can, chopped
　　and drained
1 large onion, finely chopped
2 cloves garlic, minced
½ sweet red or green pepper, chopped
⅛ t. paprika
　　Several sprigs parsley, minced
2 c. chicken broth
1½ c. long-grain rice
2 t. salt (about)
¼ t. pepper
¼ t. ground Spanish saffron
⅔ lb. shelled and deveined raw shrimp
½ 10-oz. pkg. frozen peas, thawed
12 scrubbed, unshelled clams, steamed
　　Pimiento strips
　　Chopped parsley

Heat oil in large heavy skillet or Paella pan. Add chicken seasoned with 1 teaspoon salt and ¼ teaspoon pepper. Brown well on all sides. Remove from pan or, if using Paella pan, push to one side. Add tomatoes, onion, garlic, red or green pepper, paprika and minced parsley. Sauté until onion is golden and all liquid evaporates, stirring constantly. Pour in chicken broth, rice, 2 teaspoons salt, ¼ teaspoon pepper and ground saffron; stir and bring to boil. Arrange chicken and rice in skillet or casserole about 14 inches in diameter and about 2 inches deep or arrange in Paella pan. Bake in preheated 400° oven about 30 minutes or until all liquid is absorbed by rice and grains are tender. Do not stir. During last 15 minutes add shrimp, pressing down into rice; sprinkle peas over top. When done, remove from oven; cover lightly with foil and let rest 5 minutes. Garnish with steamed clams, pressed into rice, pimiento strips and chopped parsley.

To steam clams: Place about 1 inch water in deep pot; bring to boil. Add clams; cover and steam 5 to 6 minutes or until shells open. Remove from liquid.

8 servings
Can be frozen

NOTE: Rice should be moist but not soupy. If rice is too dry add more hot bouillon. When adding clams, shrimp, cod or ham and vegetables near the end, be sure to push them down into the rice. Paella can be varied many ways. Use lobster tails, fish, duck, sausages, salami, etc.

GARLIC BREAD SLICES
Prepare & Serve: ½ hour

1 loaf Italian or French bread
½ c. soft butter
1 clove garlic, minced
½ t. oregano, crushed
½ t. dried dillweed, crushed

Cut bread crosswise into 1-inch slices. Blend together butter, garlic, oregano and dillweed. Spread over slices of bread. Put slices together in original shape; wrap in foil. Bake in preheated 400° oven for 15 to 20 minutes or until bread is crusty. Bread may be spread with butter mixture, wrapped and chilled until ready to bake.

8 servings
Can be frozen

SPANISH STYLE GREEN BEANS
(JUDIAS VERDES SOFRITO)
Cook & Serve: 50 minutes

1 lb. fresh green beans
Boiling water
1 t. salt
1½ T. olive oil
2 small onions, minced
1 large clove garlic, minced
1 1-lb. can whole tomatoes, chopped
  and drained, or 2 large tomatoes,
  peeled, seeded and chopped
1 t. sugar
Several sprigs parsley, minced
½ t. salt
Freshly ground pepper

Remove ends from beans; cut into 1-inch pieces. Drop in small amount of boiling water with 1 teaspoon salt. Cook until barely tender, about 20 minutes. Drain in colander and set aside while preparing sauce. Heat oil in 10-inch skillet. Add onions and garlic; sauté until golden, about 5 minutes. Stir in prepared tomatoes, sugar, parsley, salt and pepper. Cook uncovered until liquid evaporates and mixture is thick. Stir in beans and heat through.

6 to 8 servings
Can be frozen

SANGRIA
(WINE AND FRUIT PUNCH)
Prepare: 20 minutes
Chill: 2 hours

½ bottle dry red wine (Zinfandel)
½ bottle dry white wine (Chablis)
½ lemon (halved lengthwise)
½ orange
¼ c. brandy
1 stick cinnamon
2 10-oz. bottles club soda, chilled

Pour wine into large bowl or pitcher. Cut lemon into thin slices. Cut orange into thin slices, then cut each slice in half or cut lemon and orange in small pieces. Add fruit to wine, along with brandy and cinnamon stick. Stir to mix well. If you prefer a sweeter sangria, stir in ⅓ cup very fine sugar. Chill about 2 hours. Just before serving pour in soda and stir. Pour into chilled wine glasses with or without ice cubes.

8 servings
Cannot be frozen

CARAMEL CUSTARD
(CARAMEL FLAN)
Mix & Bake: 1¾ hours
Chill: 2 hours

½ c. granulated sugar
5 eggs
¾ c. granulated sugar
¼ t. salt
1 t. vanilla
3½ c. milk

Caramelize ½ cup sugar by cooking it in a large heavy skillet over very low heat, stirring constantly, until it is melted and golden brown. Stir with a wooden spoon and cook just until sugar melts to a golden syrup. If temperature is too high, syrup will be dark and taste burned. Immediately pour syrup into bottom of 5-cup ring mold tilting mold while syrup is liquid to also coat sides. Let cool; caramel will harden.

In a large bowl, beat eggs, sugar, salt, vanilla and milk with wire whisk. Beat until smooth but not frothy. If desired, you may strain mixture through sieve. Pour into caramel-lined ring mold or use a 5-cup shallow casserole. (To avoid spilling reserve 1 cup of egg mixture to pour into mold after it is in the oven.) Place mold in shallow baking pan in middle of oven. Pour in remaining egg mixture. Pour 1 inch of hot water into baking pan. Bake in preheated 325° oven about 1 hour and 10 minutes or until a silver knife inserted near center comes out clean. Do not overbake. Remove mold from hot water; chill at least 2 hours. Custard will settle on cooling. Unmold by running spatula around edge. Place serving platter on top of mold and turn the two upside down. Spoon some of the caramel sauce over each serving.

8 servings
Cannot be frozen

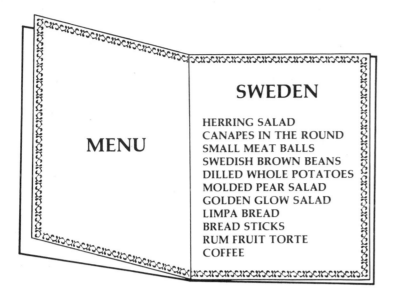

MENU

SWEDEN

HERRING SALAD
CANAPES IN THE ROUND
SMALL MEAT BALLS
SWEDISH BROWN BEANS
DILLED WHOLE POTATOES
MOLDED PEAR SALAD
GOLDEN GLOW SALAD
LIMPA BREAD
BREAD STICKS
RUM FRUIT TORTE
COFFEE

HERRING SALAD
(SILLSALLAD)
Prepare: 30 minutes
Chill: 1 hour

- 1⅔ c. diced pickled herring
- ½ c. diced red apple (with skin)
- 3 T. minced onion
- 2 medium potatoes, cooked and diced
- 1 1-lb. can diced beets, drained
- ¼ c. diced dill pickle
- 2 T. sugar
- 2 T. water
- 2 T. white wine vinegar
- ⅛ t. pepper
- ½ c. dairy sour cream
  Parsley

Place herring, apple, onion, potatoes, beets and pickle in large bowl. Mix together sugar, water, vinegar and pepper. Add to herring mixture. Fold in sour cream, mix lightly. Chill. To serve: Drain liquid. Mound on glass platter; garnish with parsley.

8 to 12 servings
Cannot be frozen

DILLED WHOLE POTATOES
Prepare & Serve: 40 minutes

- 3 lbs. new potatoes
- 1 t. salt
- ½ c. butter
- 2 t. snipped fresh dill or ½ t. dried dill weed

Pare potatoes; cook in boiling salted water until tender, about 20 minutes; drain. Sprinkle with salt; toss gently with butter until potatoes are coated evenly. Sprinkle with fresh dill weed.

8 to 10 servings
Can be frozen

SMALL MEATBALLS
(KÖTTBULLAR)
Prepare, Chill & Cook: 2 hours

- 3 slices dry toasted bread
- ½ c. boiling water
- 1¾ lbs. finely ground beef
- ¼ lb. finely ground pork shoulder
- 1 small onion, minced
- 2 eggs
  Parsley, minced
- 2 t. salt
- ¼ t. black pepper
- ⅛ t. allspice
  Pinch of ground cloves
- 2 T. butter
- 2 T. vegetable oil

Cover toast with boiling water; let stand until moistened. Add to meat with onion, eggs, parsley, salt, pepper, allspice and cloves; mix thoroughly. Shape into small balls, ¾-inch in diameter, dusting hands with flour while shaping balls. Arrange meatballs on a large baking sheet; chill 1 hour before frying. To fry meatballs: Melt butter and oil in 12-inch skillet. Add meatballs; brown slowly, shaking pan occasionally to brown on all sides. When all are browned, cover pan; steam 30 minutes. Serve hot. If making meatballs in advance, keep warm in 200° oven in casserole.

About 150 tiny meatballs
Can be frozen

NOTE: For Smörgasbord meatballs are served without sauce. If meatballs are to be served as a main course, make them larger and serve with a cream sauce

For Cream Sauce: Pour off all fat in pan, reserving drippings in pan. Stir in 1 tablespoon flour; quickly stir in ¾ cup light cream or whipping cream. Bring to boil and boil sauce over medium heat about 3 minutes; stir constantly until thick and smooth. Serve over meatballs and noodles.

Pictured opposite
Small Meatballs
Rum Fruit Torte
Dilled Whole Potatoes
Breadsticks

CANAPES IN THE ROUND (VARSMÖRGASAR)
Prepare & Serve: 45 minutes

1 slice round rye bread, about 8 inches across and ½-inch thick
2 T. soft butter
   Minced parsley
6 pimiento-stuffed olives, chopped

Spread bread with butter. In center of slice spread Cream Cheese Spread. Next spread a wide circle of Kippered Herring Spread. Make an outer border using Deviled Egg Spread. Garnish outer edges of cheese and egg mixtures with minced parsley and the outer edge of the herring mixture with chopped stuffed olives. Cut into wedges for serving.

12 wedges
Cannot be frozen

CREAM CHEESE SPREAD

1½ t. chopped pimiento
1 3-oz. pkg. cream cheese

Add pimiento to cheese; mix well.

KIPPERED HERRING SPREAD

1 3¼-oz. can Kippered herring
1 T. lemon juice
3 T. salad dressing

Remove bones from herring; mash. Add remaining ingredients; mix well.

DEVILED EGG SPREAD

2 hard-cooked eggs
2 T. salad dressing
½ t. prepared mustard

Mash cooked eggs with fork; add salad dressing and mustard. Blend well.

GOLDEN GLOW SALAD
Prepare: 15 minutes
Chill: 4 hours

1¾ c. boiling water
1 3-oz. pkg. lemon flavored gelatin
¼ t. salt
⅔ c. diced canned pineapple, drained
2 carrots, grated
   Mayonnaise

Pour boiling water over gelatin; stir to dissolve gelatin. Add salt. Let stand until slightly thickened. Fold in well-drained pineapple and grated carrots. Pour into oiled 3½ cup mold. Chill; unmold and serve with mayonnaise.

About 12 servings
Cannot be frozen

MOLDED PEAR SALAD
Prepare: 15 minutes
Chill: 4 hours

1½ c. boiling water
1 3-oz. pkg. raspberry flavored gelatin
¼ c. lemon juice
2 c. diced pears
   Mayonnaise

Pour boiling water over gelatin; stir until gelatin is dissolved; add lemon juice. Set aside until slightly thickened. Fold in pears. Pour into oiled 3½ cup mold; chill. Unmold; serve with mayonnaise.

About 12 servings
Cannot be frozen

SWEDISH BROWN BEANS (BRUNA BÖNAR)
Soak: Overnight
Cook & Serve: About 2¼ hours

1 lb. brown or navy beans
7 c. water
¾ c. firmly packed brown sugar
¾ c. dark corn syrup
⅓ c. vinegar
2 t. salt
¼ t. nutmeg
1 t. cornstarch
2 T. cold water

Wash and drain beans. Add 7 cups water; cover and let stand overnight. In morning bring to boil; reduce heat. Cover; simmer about 2 hours, or until done. Add sugar, syrup, vinegar, salt and nutmeg. Mix cornstarch and 2 tablespoons cold water; stir into beans. Simmer uncovered 15 minutes. Serve hot.

8 servings
Can be frozen

RUM FRUIT TORTE
(FRUKT KAKA)
Bake & Serve: 2 hours

    4 egg yolks
    ⅔ c. sugar
    ¼ c. water
    1 t. vanilla
    ¼ t. almond extract
    ⅔ c. sifted cake flour
    ¾ t. baking powder
    ¼ t. salt
    4 egg whites, stiffly beaten
       Rum Filling
       Sliced peaches
       Sliced strawberries
  1½ c. whipping cream, whipped

Beat yolks until thick and light in color. Beat in sugar gradually. Add water, vanilla and almond extract; beat until well mixed. Sift together flour, baking powder and salt. Fold into first mixture using wire whisk. Then using rubber spatula fold in stiffly beaten egg whites. Turn into ungreased 9-inch spring form or tube pan. Bake in preheated 325° oven 50 to 55 minutes. Remove from oven, turn upside down on cake rack; cool. When cold, remove from pan. Cut into 3 equal layers. Place one layer on cake platter. Spread with half of Rum Filling; top with sliced peaches. Place second layer on top of peaches; spread with remaining Rum Filling. Top with sliced strawberries. Place third layer on top of strawberries. Cover top layer and sides with whipped cream. Garnish with sliced peaches and strawberries. Serve immediately or chill before serving time.

10 servings
Cannot be frozen

RUM FILLING

    2 t. unflavored gelatin
    2 T. cold water
    ½ c. milk
    2 egg yolks
    ⅓ c. sugar
    3 T. rum
    ¼ t. vanilla
       Dash salt
    ½ c. whipping cream, whipped
    1 egg white, stiffly beaten

Soak gelatin in cold water. Scald milk, add soaked gelatin and stir until gelatin is dis-

solved. Beat egg yolks slightly, add sugar and mix well. Stir in hot milk mixture. Add rum, vanilla and salt. Chill until slightly thickened. Fold in whipped cream then the stiffly beaten egg white. Let stand until almost set.

SWEDISH RYE BREAD
(LIMPA BREAD)
Mix, Shape & Bake: 3¾ hours

    5 to 5½ c. self-rising flour
    2 pkgs. dry yeast
    2 c. water
    ½ c. firmly-packed light brown sugar
    2 T. vegetable oil
    2 t. grated orange rind
    1 t. anise seed
  1½ t. fennel seed
    2 eggs
    2 c. rye flour
       Oil

Stir together 3 cups flour and yeast. Boil water, sugar, 2 tablespoons oil, orange rind, anise and fennel seeds 3 minutes. Cool to lukewarm; add to flour-yeast mixture and beat until smooth, about 2 minutes using medium speed. Blend in eggs. Add 1 cup self-rising flour; beat 1 minute using medium speed. Stir in rye flour and more self-rising flour to make a moderately stiff dough. Turn onto lightly floured surface; knead until smooth and elastic, about 8 to 10 minutes. Shape into ball; place in lightly greased bowl. Twirl to grease all sides. Cover; let rise in warm place (80 to 85°) until doubled, about 1½ hours. Punch down. Divide dough in half; shape into balls. Let rest 10 minutes. Shape loaves. Place in 2 greased 4½ x 8½-inch loaf pans; brush with oil. Let rise in warm place until doubled, about 1 hour. Bake in preheated 400° oven 35 minutes, or until done. If necessary, cover with aluminum foil to prevent excess browning. Remove from pans immediately; brush with oil.

To shape loaves: Roll dough into rectangle 9 inches wide. Starting at 9-inch end roll jelly-roll fashion. Seal seam. With side of hand, press ends to seal. Fold ends under loaf. Place in pan, seam side down.

2 loaves
Can be frozen

Shish Kebab with Pilaf

Lamb with Pilaf

MENU

TURKEY

RICE FILLED VINE LEAVES
SHISH KEBAB WITH PILAFF
or
LAMB WITH PILAFF
CUCUMBER SALAD
FARINA DESSERT
TURKISH COFFEE

RICE-FILLED VINE LEAVES
(YALANCI DOLMA)
Prepare & Serve: 3 hours

1 c. rice
  Warm water
¾ c. vegetable oil
1 lb. onions, minced
¼ c. fresh dill or 1 T. dried dillweed
½ c. minced parsley
¼ c. fresh mint or 1 T. dried mint leaves
2 t. salt
¼ t. pepper
¼ t. oregano
3 T. lemon juice
1 T. tomato sauce
3 c. boiling water
1 jar vine leaves

Place rice in bowl; add enough warm water to cover. Let stand 5 minutes. Put ¾ cup oil in large skillet. Add onions and dill; sauté until golden. Add drained rice, parsley, mint, salt, pepper, oregano, lemon juice and tomato sauce. Cook about 5 minutes, stirring occasionally. Add 1 cup boiling water; cook, stirring occasionally, until all water is absorbed. Remove from heat. Rinse vine leaves with cold water. Place leaf (smooth or shiny side) on board. Put about 1 teaspoon rice filling in center of each leaf. Fold ends toward center and gently roll tight like jelly roll. In large roasting pan, carefully place stuffed leaves side by side, then in layers. Pour remaining oil and boiling water over top of leaves. Cover with additional leaves.

Place plate on top to hold leaves in place while cooking. Cover pan and bring to boil on top of range. Remove from heat and place in preheated 350° oven 25 to 30 minutes or until done. Cool; serve warm or cold. May be made a day in advance and warmed before serving.

About 120 Sarmas
Can be frozen

Rice-filled Vine Leaves

CUCUMBER SALAD
(CACIK)
Prepare: 15 minutes
Let Stand: 30 minutes

2 medium cucumbers
1 t. salt
1 c. yogurt or sour cream
1 small clove garlic, pressed
  Fresh dill, snipped

Peel and thinly slice cucumbers. Sprinkle with salt; let stand 30 minutes. Drain excess moisture from cucumbers by pressing lightly against side of bowl. Toss with yogurt and garlic. Sprinkle with fresh dill.

6 servings
Cannot be frozen

SHISH KEBAB WITH PILAF
Marinate: 4 hours
Prepare & Serve: 45 minutes

- 2 lbs. lean lamb
- 1 clove garlic, minced
- ½ c. olive oil
  Juice of 2 lemons
- 2 t. salt
- ⅛ t. pepper
- 2 t. oregano
- 1 medium onion
- 1 bay leaf
- 2 large green peppers
- ½ c. boiling water
  Mushroom caps, 1½ inches in diameter
  (reserve stems for Pilaf)
- 3 tomatoes, quartered or cherry tomatoes

Trim fat from meat and cut into 1½-inch cubes. Place in shallow pan. Combine garlic with oil, lemon juice, salt, pepper and oregano. Beat with fork and pour over meat cubes. Slice onion into rings; add to meat with bay leaf. Cover; chill about 4 hours. Cut peppers lengthwise into thirds and clean. Drop into boiling water for 1 minute. Remove; cut again in thirds crosswise. Alternate meat, green pepper, mushroom caps and tomatoes on spits, placing spits lengthwise through stem section of mushroom caps. Brush with marinade. Broil or cook on outdoor grill about 15 minutes over medium heat, then over high heat for 7 minutes or until meat is done. Baste frequently.

6 servings
Cannot be frozen

PILAF
(PILAV)
Cook & Serve: 1 hour

- 1 T. butter
- ¼ t. rosemary, crushed
  Reserved mushroom stems from Shish Kebabs, chopped
- 3 c. water
- 1 chicken bouillon cube
- 1 t. salt
- 1½ c. long grain rice
- ⅓ c. butter

Melt 1 tablespoon butter. Add rosemary and mushroom stems; brown 3 to 4 minutes. Bring water to boil; add bouillon cube and salt. Stir until dissolved. Wash rice; drain. Melt butter in saucepan. Add rice; heat 6 minutes or until butter is absorbed. Gradually add broth. Cover; simmer 15 minutes. Add rosemary, butter and mushroom stems. Stir 5 minutes over low heat. Cover; let stand 25 minutes. Serve immediately.

6 servings
Can be frozen

PILAF WITH LAMB
(KUZULU PILAV)
Prepare & Serve: 45 minutes

- 1 c. long grain rice
- 3 T. butter or margarine
- 2 green onions, sliced
- 2 c. chicken broth
- ¾ t. salt
- ¾ c. pitted ripe olives, chopped
  Few sprigs parsley, minced
- 4 loin lamb chops
- 2 T. lemon juice
- 2 t. oregano
  Salt
- 4 tomato wedges
  Whole pitted ripe olives for garnish

Brown rice slowly in butter, stirring frequently, until golden. Add onion and cook a minute longer. Add broth, ¾ teaspoon salt, chopped olives and parsley; heat to boiling. Cover; cook over low heat 20 minutes, or until rice is tender and liquid is absorbed. Meanwhile brush lamb chops with lemon juice and sprinkle with oregano. When rice is done, broil chops about 4 inches from heat for 8 to 10 minutes on each side. Sprinkle with salt. Mound rice on serving platter, and surround with lamb chops. Garnish with tomato wedges and whole ripe olives.

4 servings
Can be frozen

FARINA DESSERT
(HALVA)
Cook & Serve: 45 minutes

¾ c. butter	4 c. water
2 c. farina	2 c. sugar
1 c. chopped almonds	Cinnamon

Melt butter; add farina and almonds. Cook, stirring constantly, until golden. Bring water and sugar to boil; slowly pour boiling hot into farina mixture, stirring constantly until liquid is absorbed and it can be shaped into a ball. Let cool 5 minutes. Turn into 5-cup mold or individual small forms, or serve in dessert plates by spoonfuls. Sprinkle with cinnamon before serving.

10 servings
Can be frozen

TURKISH COFFEE
(CAFE)
Prepare & Serve: 10 minutes

1 c. cold water
2 T. sugar
4 t. pulverized coffee

Put water in "jezve," a cylindrical copper pot with long handle, or use a small saucepan. Add sugar and coffee. Stir well. Heat to rising boil. Remove from heat. Pour off froth into cups. Bring coffee to boil again. Fill cups. Serve immediately.

4 demitasse cups

BARLEY SOUP
(YAYLA TSHORBASI)
Cook & Serve: 30 Minutes

2 T. butter
1 medium onion, chopped
1 c. quick-cooking barley
2 qts. water
2 t. salt
1 c. yogurt or dairy sour cream

Melt butter in Dutch oven. Sauté onion until golden. Add water and bring to boil. Add barley and salt. Cook until tender, about 10 to 12 minutes. Stir small amount of the hot mixture into yogurt or sour cream, then return to Dutch oven. Keep warm over very low heat. Serve immediately.

8 servings
Can be frozen

HOMEMADE YOGURT
(YAYOURTI)
Prepare: 45 minutes
Let Stand: 5 hours

¼ c. nonfat dry milk solids
1 qt. milk, 2%, skim or regular
2 to 4 T. commercial or natural yogurt

Stir milk solids into milk. Heat to 185° using candy thermometer. Cool to 115°. Mix a little hot milk into yogurt, then stir mixture into milk. Pour into 1-quart pyrex or earthenware bowl or 2 widemouthed pint jars; cover. Incubate about 5 hours by wrapping a blanket around the containers or placing in the oven on warm setting. Temperature for incubation should be about 113°. Do not disturb. Refrigerate: Yogurt will keep in the refrigerator 6 to 7 days.

1 quart Yogurt
Cannot be frozen

YOGURT DRINK
(ARYAN)
Mix & Serve: 5 minutes

1 c. yogurt	3 c. ice water

Beat together yogurt and water. Serve immediately or refrigerate; stir before serving.

4 servings
Cannot be frozen

WHAT WINES AND WHICH FOODS

These are proper wine and food combinations. Remember, however, that there are no rules! The "correct" wine is the one you like best.

FOOD	WINES	SERVING TEMPERATURE
	APPETIZER WINES	
Hors d'oeuvres	SHERRY (*dry or medium*)	Serve chilled at
Nuts	FRUIT-FLAVORED WINES	cocktail time
Cheeses	VERMOUTH (*dry or sweet*)	
	RED DINNER WINES	
	BURGUNDY (*dry*)	
Steaks	Gamay (*gah-may'*)	
Chops	Petite Sirah (*pet-eet sear-ah*)	
Roasts	Pinot Noir (*pea-no no-ahr'*)	Serve at cool room
Game		temperature (65°)
Cheese Dishes	CLARET (*dry*)	
Spaghetti	Cabernet Sauvignon (*so-vee-nyonh*)	
Lamb	Ruby Cabernet (ruby *kab-er-nay'*)	
	Zinfandel (*zin'-fan-dell*)	
	OTHERS	
	Barbera (*bar-bair'-a*) (*dry*)	
	Red Chianti (*kee-ahn'-tee*) (*dry*)	
	Concord (*sweet*)	
Rosé—true "go-with-anything" wine, except delicate fish dishes, extremely heavy casseroles and game dishes	ROSÉ (*pink*) (*roh-zay'*) (dry to slightly sweet)	Serve Rosé chilled
	WHITE DINNER WINES	
	CHABLIS (*sha-blee'*) (*dry*)	
	Chardonnay or Pinot Chardonnay	
	(*pea-no shar-doh-nay'*)	
	Pinot Blanc (*pea-no blanh*)	
	Chenin Blanc (*shen-in blanh*)	
	(*dry to sweet*)	
Chicken		Serve well chilled, about
Turkey		50°—cold enough to be re-
Fish	RHINE WINE (*dry*)	freshing but not so cold
Shellfish	Emerald Riesling (*reez'-ling*)	that it kills the aroma.
Omelets	Grey Riesling	
Any white meats	Gewurztraminer (*ge-verts-tra-mee'-ner*)	
Salads	Johannisberg (er) Riesling	
Cheeses		
Sandwiches	SAUTERNE (*so-tairn'*) (*dry to sweet*)	
Light Dishes	Fume Blanc (*fou-may blanh*)	
	Sauvignon Blanc (*so-vee-nyonh blanh*)	
	Haut (*oh*) or Chateau (*shat-toh'*)	
	OTHERS	
	Light Muscat (*dry to sweet*)	
	Catawba (*dry to sweet*)	
	Delaware (*dry to semisweet*)	

Rule of thumb: the lighter the food, the lighter the wine. The more delicately seasoned the food, the drier (less sweet) the wine.

SWEET DESSERT WINES

Before dinner
After dinner
With dessert (fruits, nuts, cookies, fruit-cake, pound cake)
With cheese

PORT *(red, white or tawny)*
TOKAY *(toh-kay')*
SHERRY *(cream or sweet)*
MUSCATEL *(golden, red or black)*

Serve Port at room temperature—Tokay and Sherry chilled or at cool room temperature, Muscatel chilled.

Guideline: the lighter the snack (or earlier in the day), the lighter the wine.

SPARKLING WINES   Serve well chilled.

Serve with all foods:
Appetizers
Main course
Desserts
Festive party punches

CHAMPAGNE *(sham-pain')* *(gold or pink)*

SPARKLING BURGUNDY *(semisweet to sweet)*

COLD DUCK *(semisweet to sweet)*

SPARKLING ROSÉ *(dry to semisweet)*

Courtesy Sino Eleven Cellars Winery
Meiers Winery

INDEX

Continued

ABOUT THE AUTHOR

Sophie Kay is a vivacious, personable television personality and nationally recognized home economist. She is currently doing a cooking segment on a television show on WISN-TV in Milwaukee. Throughout the country, Sophie has lectured and conducted many cooking schools for television, radio, newspapers and women's clubs. Sophie Kay is president of the Sophie Kay Cooking School Ltd. in Milwaukee, a member of American Women in Radio and TV Broadcasting, American Home Economics Association, and is listed in Who's Who of American Women.

A very special thank you to the following for their cooperation and use of their photos: California Avocado Advisory Board, National Livestock & Meat Board, Durum Wheat Institute, National Broiler Council, Wheat Flour Institute, United Dairy Industry Association, Denmark Cheese Association, Frozen Potato Products Institute, Uncle Ben's Rice, California Ripe Olives.

OTHER COOKBOOKS AVAILABLE

All Holidays Cookbook
American Cookbook
Christmas Cookbook
Christmas Gifts from the Kitchen
Cookie Cookbook
Country Bread Cookbook
Country Kitchen
Family Cookbook
Family Favorites from Ideals
Farmhouse Cookbook
Festive Party Cookbook
From Mama's Honey Jar
From Mama's Kitchen
Garden Cookbook
Gourmet on the Go
The Gourmet Touch
Guide to Microwave Cooking
Have a Gourmet Christmas
Junior Chef Cookbook
Menus from Around the World
Naturally Nutritious
Nice and Easy Desserts
Simply Delicious
Soups for All Seasons
Tempting Treasures
Whole Grain Cookbook

Editorial Director, James Kuse

Managing Editor, Ralph Luedtke

Production Editor/Manager, Richard Lawson

Photographic Editor, Gerald Koser